W9-CAX-688

The Nano-Reef Handbook

CR Brightwell

tfh

The Nano-Reef Handbook

Project Team
Editor: Brian M. Scott
Copy Editor: Stephanie Hays
Design: Candida Tomassini, Angela Stanford
Cover Design: Mary Ann Kahn

T.F.H. Publications
President/CEO: Glen S. Axelrod
Executive Vice President: Mark E. Johnson
Publisher: Christopher T. Reggio
Production Manager: Kathy Bontz

T.F.H. Publications, Inc.
One TFH Plaza
Third and Union Avenues
Neptune City, NJ 07753

Copyright © 2006 by T.F.H. Publications, Inc.

All rights reserved. No part of this publication may be reproduced, stored, or transmitted in any form, or by any means electronic, mechanical or otherwise, without written permission from T.F.H. Publications, except where permitted by law. Requests for permission or further information should be directed to the above address.

Published and bound in China

07 08 09 10   3 5 7 9 8 6 4 2

Library of Congress Cataloging-in-Publication Data
Brightwell, Chris.
The nano-reef handbook / Chris Brightwell.
p. cm.
Includes bibliographical references and index.
ISBN 0-7938-0572-4 (alk. paper)
1. Marine aquariums. 2. Marine aquarium fishes. 3. Coral reef animals. I. Title.
SF457.1B75 2006
639.34'2--dc22
2005036095

This book has been published with the intent to provide accurate and authoritative information in regard to the subject matter within. While every reasonable precaution has been taken in preparation of this book, the author and publisher expressly disclaim responsibility for any errors, omissions, or adverse effects arising from the use or application of the information contained herein. The techniques and suggestions are used at the reader's discretion and are not to be considered a substitute for veterinary care. If you suspect a medical problem, consult your veterinarian.

The Leader In Responsible Animal Care For Over 50 Years!™
www.tfhpublications.com

Dedication

To my mother, for always encouraging me to do my best and follow my dreams, and for always being supportive of my decisions.

Acknowledgments

Though I have been an avid aquarium hobbyist for many years and earned a degree in marine science that has undoubtedly contributed to my understanding of the complexities of closed marine aquaria, I would likely have never gotten the experience needed to write such a thorough book as this were if not for Jack Kent hiring me in an exploratory role as marine scientist at Kent Marine in February of 2000. Therefore, my sincere thanks go out to him for having the vision and faith that enabled me to develop my knowledge base more fully. Much of the development of my understanding of aquarium husbandry has been encouraged by the countless hobbyists with whom I have conversed over the past several years—my thanks to you all.

In preparation for setting up numerous nano-reefs to photograph in this book, several representatives from companies in the aquarium industry stepped forward and generously offered to provide me with their products and services. They are, in no particular order, Bryan Moore from Milwaukee Instruments, Inc., Jason Kim from AquaC, Inc., Rick Amour from That Fish Place, Ian Poole from Kent Marine, Gary Sparks from Energy Savers Unlimited, Ike Eigenbrode from Current USA, Matt Allen from All-Glass Aquarium, and Am'thyst Sloan from CPR Aquatics. Your generous contributions were much appreciated—my heartfelt thanks to you all.

And last, but certainly not least, I would like to thank Dr. Robert Young, Dr. Daniel Abel, Dr. Susan Libes, and Dr. Craig Gilman, four of my "regular" professors at Coastal Carolina University, with whom I spent many years learning the ropes of marine science as an undergraduate. I could never have gotten here without your patience and support.

Table of Contents

Testing the Waters:
Is a Nano-Reef Right for You?

In this day and age of downsizing, it seems inevitable that tiny aquaria would eventually become a reality of the reef hobby. What's somewhat surprising is that these aquaria have been accepted with open arms by a hobby that heretofore has operated under the motto, "Bigger is better." While many hobbyists fall asleep every night dreaming of the massive (i.e., swimming pool-sized) reef system they plan to install in their home one day, an ever-growing number of hobbyists, both experienced and inexperienced, try their hand at aquaria under 15 gallons (57 l) in total volume, some even less than 7 gallons (26 l)! These small systems have been given the moniker "**nano-reef**" aquaria, with nano- from the Greek *nanos*, meaning dwarf.

Ironically, these tiny aquaria are often the envy of "big tank" hobbyists for a number of reasons. First, the smaller an aquarium is, the less money is required to set it up with the proper equipment. Second, less water volume means that less livestock, live rock, and live sand is needed to make the aquarium appear full and natural, which in turn means that the aquarium can be completely stocked for a more reasonable amount of money than a larger system. Third, smaller aquaria cost less to operate per unit time due to the relatively modest array of electrical components required. Fourth, the smaller an aquarium is, the less space it requires, which is very important to those hobbyists living in small spaces, such as city apartments and dormitories. Hobbyists wishing to have a "place to get away" while at their desk may do so with a small aquarium; the first aquarium I was allowed to set up in my office after graduating college was a 15-gallon reef (57-l). Fifth, smaller aquaria typically produce less noise than larger systems, an important consideration for hobbyists wishing to set a reef up in a location where excessive noise is undesirable, such as in a bedroom, waiting room, or office.

Experienced hobbyists will attest that no matter which way you look at it, larger systems have a number of advantages over relatively smaller systems. The first major difference is that stability of water parameters increases with water volume; that is to say, the more water present in the aquarium system, the less fluctuation in parameters such as pH, alkalinity, ammonia, etc., will occur per unit time. Marine organisms have evolved under very stable chemical conditions and are rarely exposed to drastic fluctuations in chemistry over short periods of time. Therefore, the greater the degree of fluctuation, the greater the negative impact on marine livestock, so the greater the need to understand marine aquarium husbandry before making any purchases becomes. It's certainly feasible to envision a scenario in which a hobbyist spends hundreds (or even thousands) of dollars over the course of a year continually replacing livestock that has perished in a small aquarium due to unstable water chemistry. Theoretically, they could have spent the same amount of money completely stocking a larger aquarium system and suffering no loss of life.

Keeping this in mind, it can be stated that a smaller aquarium doesn't necessarily cost the hobbyist less money in the long run than a larger system, but this is an unlikely contingency.

Let's examine the scenario presented above and the impact it has on two hobbyists, one an experienced reef-keeper, the other a novice. The experienced hobbyist has set up and maintained all manner of aquaria over a period of several years, probably owns two or more systems of 50 gallons (189 l) or greater total volume, understands marine water chemistry well enough to know how to balance the parameters within the desired ranges, is familiar with the role of various methods of filtration, and can identify and correct problems before they become lethal to livestock either by looking at the appearance of the livestock itself or performing regular water testing with accurate test kits.

This person can overcome the inherent difficulties, and therefore has a very good chance of being successful, with a truly small aquarium. The novice, on the other hand, may have never owned a marine aquarium before, or perhaps they have a slightly larger system of 20–30 gallons (76-114 l) with a few pieces of live rock and some fish that has been set up for a few weeks or months. Though they've read a great deal in books and periodicals, they haven't yet made the mistakes or spent the time necessary to really understand the dynamics of marine aquarium husbandry. Therefore, they are unable to balance things as well as they'd like, and the occasional loss of a fish or invertebrate is just water under the bridge of experience. To this person, a nano-reef may wind up costing a lot of money and time, and leaves a bad taste for the hobby in the neophyte's mouth. These points are not made to be overly dramatic, nor to dissuade the novice from setting up a nano-reef; they are meant to illustrate the challenges that a small reef aquarium poses to a hobbyist of *any* experience level.

> **Nano-Note**
> Nano is the metric system prefix for 1×10^{-9}, or one billionth (1/1,000,000,000) of a whole unit.

Weigh the pros and cons, and then ask yourself if a nano-reef is right for you. The first step to perform, before making any equipment purchases, is to read as much credible information on the subject of nano-reef setup, stocking, and long-term maintenance as you can find. Reading cannot be completely substituted for bona fide experience, however it *can* help you make the right initial decisions and recognize and correct problems before they get out of hand. This guide will be part of your education. I suggest that you read the entire book, cover to cover, at least twice before you spend one nickel on the aquarium itself. Take your time, make notes and highlight sections in this book, and ask questions of those experienced nano-reefers you're acquainted with. Let's get down to business…

The Nano-Reef System

9

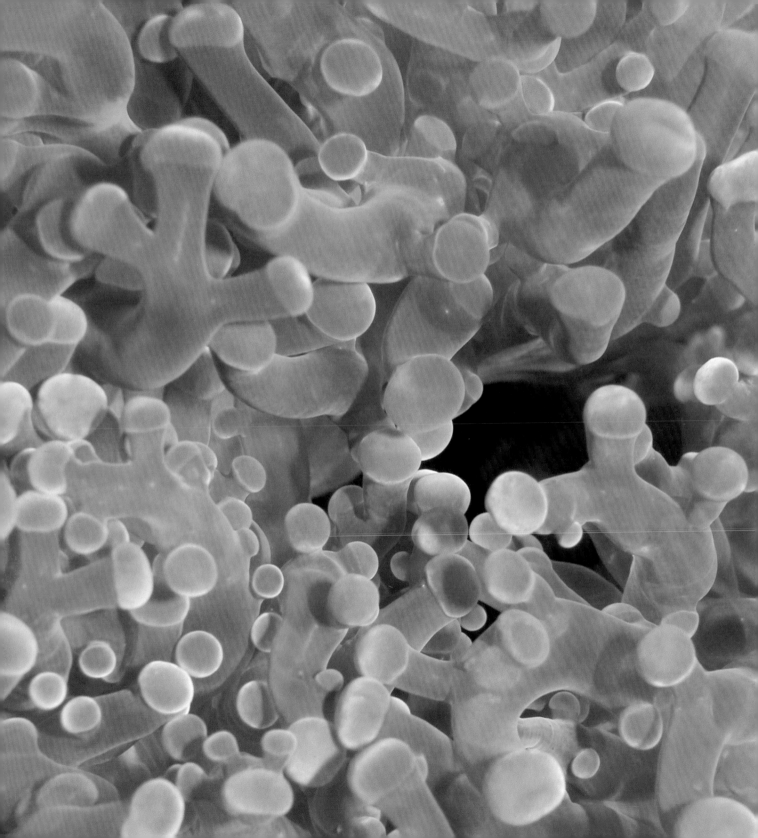

Chapter One

Water Quality:
The First Key to Success

You will undoubtedly find that the most important aspect of maintaining any aquarium is water quality. More specifically, it can be stated that unless water parameters are maintained within the proper ranges for the livestock in the aquarium, no amount of filtration, lighting, or other support equipment will make up for it. Aquatic organisms have spent several million years evolving under conditions that change very little from day to day. They rely on the unchanging chemical makeup of the water to provide them with the necessary elements and nutrients for proper function. If the water chemistry fails to meet the requirements, the organisms begin to suffer, eventually perishing. To understand water chemistry, it is important to lay down a foundation of terminology; this will help you better understand why it is necessary to pay special attention to certain parameters and not worry so much about others.

Defining the Terminology

Salt water, or sea water as it will be referred to throughout the remainder of this book, is rather complex in nature. It is comprised of water and varying concentrations of every naturally occurring element known. Many of these elements exist in sea water as ions and/or constituents of dissolved and particulate molecules, while others may exist as gases. The elements are separated into three general groups: major, minor, and trace elements. Table 1.1 lists the major, minor, and trace elements as well as their approximate concentrations in sea water. Note that major elements constitute over 99.9% of the total dissolved salts present in the oceans.

Table 1.1. Average Natural Seawater Concentrations of Elements

Atomic #	Common Name	Element	Molecular Weight	Concentration (ppm)
1	Hydrogen	H (as H2O)	1.00790	055.79E+03
2	Helium	He	4.00260	007.38E-06
3	Lithium	Li	6.94100	177.86E-03
4	Beryllium	Be	9.01210	600.44E-09
5	Boron	B	10.81000	004.65E+00
6	Carbon	C (organic)	12.01100	049.25E-03
7	Nitrogen	N (as NO^3.)	14.00670	430.71E-03
8	Oxygen	O2 (gas)	15.99940	003.61E+00
9	Fluorine	F	18.99840	001.32E+00
10	Neon	Ne	20.17900	155.13E-06
11	Sodium	Na	22.98980	011.08E+03
12	Magnesium	Mg	24.30500	001.32E+03
13	Aluminum	Al	26.98150	829.68E-06
14	Silicon	Si	28.05500	002.88E+00
15	Phosphorus	P	30.97380	073.02E-03
16	Sulfur	S	32.06000	920.12E+00
17	Chlorine	Cl	35.45300	019.99E+03
18	Argon	Ar	39.94800	614.20E-03
19	Potassium	K	39.09830	408.77E+00
20	Calcium	Ca	40.08000	423.14E+00
21	Scandium	Sc	44.95590	691.20E-09
22	Titanium	Ti	47.88000	981.54E-06
23	Vanadium	V	50.94150	001.20E-03
24	Chromium	Cr	51.9960	213.18E-06
25	Manganese	Mn	54.9380	281.56E-06
26	Iron	Fe	55.8470	057.24E-06
27	Cobalt	Co	58.9332	001.81E-06
28	Nickel	Ni	58.6900	481.26E-06
29	Copper	Cu	63.5460	260.54E-06
30	Zinc	Zn	65.3900	402.15E-06

Table 1.1. Average Natural Seawater Concentrations of Elements cont.

Atomic #	Common Name	Element	Molecular Weight	Concentration (ppm)
31	Galium	Ga	69.7200	021.44E-06
32	Germanium	Ge	72.5900	005.21E-06
33	Arsenic	As	74.9216	001.77E-03
34	Selenium	Se	78.9600	137.59E-06
35	Bromine	Br	79.9040	068.80E+00
36	Krypton	Kr	83.8000	292.04E-06
37	Rubidium	Rb	85.4678	122.65E-03
38	Strontium	Sr	87.6200	007.81E+00
39	Yttrium	Y	88.9059	013.67E-06
40	Zirconium	Zr	91.2250	028.05E-06
41	Niobium	Nb	92.9064	004.76E-06
42	Molybdenum	Mo	95.9400	010.82E-03
43	Technetium	Tc	98.0000	000.00E+00
44	Ruthenium	Ru	101.0700	000.00E+00
45	Rhodium	Rh	102.9060	000.00E+00
46	Paladium	Pd	106.4200	000.00E+00
47	Silver	Ag	107.8680	002.76E-06
48	Cadmium	Cd	112.4100	080.65E-06
49	Indium	In	114.8200	117.69E-09
50	Tin	Sn	118.7100	486.71E-09
51	Antimony	Sb	121.7500	149.75E-06
52	Tellurium	Te	127.6000	000.00E+00
53	Iodine	I	126.9050	057.23E-03
54	Xenon	Xe	131.2900	067.29E-06
55	Cesium	Cs	132.9050	299.70E-06
56	Barium	Ba	137.3300	014.08E-03
57	Lanthanum	La	138.9060	004.27E-06

It is important to maintain the natural seawater concentration of calcium in all aquaria housing corals and their allies. While some corals, such as the Zoanthids shown here, utilize relatively little calcium compared to their distant stony cousins, it is still important to monitor the calcium concentration in their aquaria.

- **Major Elements** are those elements that exist in a concentration that is greater than or equal to one part per million (ppm) by weight.
- **Minor elements** exist in concentrations of less than one ppm but greater than one part per billion (ppb).
- **Trace elements** are present in concentrations less than or equal to one ppb.

One can also categorize elements in terms of their tendency to undergo chemical and/or biological interaction. If an organism utilizes an element in some fashion (i.e., in a biological function), the concentration of the element is subject to gradual depletion as conditions warrant. These elements are said to behave **non-conservatively**. One might think that calcium would fall into this category. It is utilized by various groups of organisms, such as corals (anthozoans), clams and scallops (bivalves), snails (gastropods), and marine algae such as *Halimeda* sp. and *Penicillus* sp. to form skeletal mass. However, because the total amount of calcium in sea water far exceeds the amount removed by these and other organisms, the concentration doesn't deplete; rather, it is constantly replenished by sea water from other parts of the globe. Due to this special circumstance, calcium is also considered a **bio-intermediate** element. Other non-conservative elements and solutes include silica, carbon, minor and trace elements, gases, nutrients, and organic compounds.

Elements that are not utilized by living organisms are said to behave **conservatively**; that is, the concentration of these elements will not become depleted as a result of interaction with living organisms. Another term used to describe these elements is **bio-unlimiting**.

Nutrients are substances required by plants for growth. Silica, phosphate, and nitrate are the three nutrients of concern in a marine aquarium. Adequate concentrations of silica will encourage the growth of **diatoms**, a group of phytoplankton that utilizes hydrated silica to create an exoskeleton. Similarly, when phosphate and nitrate reach adequate concentrations, the result is a thriving mass of **filamentous algae** and/or **cyanobacteria** (commonly referred to as "slime algae" due to its greasy, slimy appearance). All of these organisms detract from the appearance of the aquarium and can negatively impact the livestock (particularly corals and their allies) by growing over them. However, in the nano-reef it is likely that the bigger issue behind excessive phosphate and/or nitrate concentrations is poor water quality, which must not be allowed to persist if the hobbyist expects to be successful in the long term.

Elements that are rapidly depleted by biological activity are referred to as **biolimiting**, because without their presence in adequate concentrations, biological production cannot continue. In addition to the aforementioned nutrients, iron is a biolimiting element; it is required to form chlorophyll, and without it algae and other marine plants (both desirable and undesirable) cannot grow and reproduce.

Defining the Parameters

Although the average values for parameters such as pH, alkalinity, salinity, and the concentrations of the multitude of substances dissolved in sea water are fairly well defined, it is not necessary to maintain these values at *exactly* those found

Figure 1.2. Recommended Ranges of Water Parameters in a Nano-Reef Aquarium	
Temperature	72° – 78°F (22°-25°C)
Density	1.021 –1.026 g/cm^3
pH	8.1 –8.4
Alkalinity	8.0 – 12.0 dKH (3.0 – 4.5meq/L)
Calcium [Ca2+]	412.0 –450.0 ppm
Magnesium [Mg2+]	1288.0 – 1320.0 ppm
Strontium [Sr2+]	8.0 –10.0 ppm
Iron [Fe2+/3+]	0.1 –0.3 ppm
Iodine [I-, IO3-]	0.05 –0.08 ppm
Phosphate	<0.05 ppm (immeasurable)
Silicate	<0.05 ppm (immeasurable)
Ammonia [NH3]	0.0 ppm (immeasurable)
Nitrite [NO2-]	0.0 ppm (immeasurable)
Nitrate [NO3-]	<10.0 ppm

The Nano-Reef System

15

PART ONE

in natural sea water. In fact, it would be impossible to do so, particularly in a nano-reef, due to the limited amount of dissolved substances available to the livestock. Fortunately, most marine organisms are able to adjust to slight variations in water chemistry from those to which they have evolved. It is important to maintain parameters within a small range of values at all times, for although certain elements may not be utilized directly by the livestock, they may be important to reactions that maintain the long-term stability of the water chemistry itself. The closer the actual value of a parameter is to the natural seawater value, the better. However, just as important is maintaining this value within the smallest range you can manage. See Figure 1.2 for the recommended ranges of recognized important parameters in a reef aquarium.

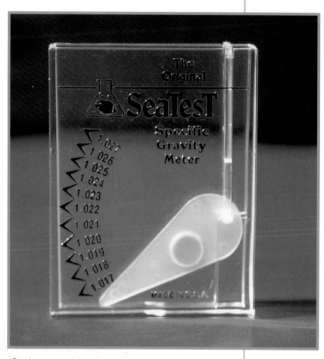

Swing-arm hydrometers, such as the one shown, provide a fast and relatively accurate reading of salinity. Refractometers are the choice of advanced hobbyists, largely because they are more expensive than swing-arm hydrometers.

The ionic strength, or sum of all dissolved substances, of the sea water is measured by oceanographers in several ways. The two that are referred to throughout aquarium literature are salinity and density. **Salinity** is measured in units of parts per thousand (ppt or ‰); sea water is approximately 3.5%, or 35‰, dissolved solids by weight. **Density** is measured in units of grams of dissolved substance per ml of sea water; the average specific gravity of sea water is approximately 1.024 g/cm^3. This means that sea water is approximately 1.024 times as dense as pure fresh water.

The basis of any successful reef aquarium is purified fresh water and a quality synthetic salt mix; this is particularly the case for a nano-reef. By using water that has had all dissolved substances stripped from it, the hobbyist has a clean slate to work with and can start with *exactly* what he or she needs without worrying about the presence of phosphate, silicate, and nitrate (not to mention chlorine, chloramines, and heavy metals), which are often present in tap water, particularly in agricultural or resort areas. Nano-reef aquaria are small enough that purchasing gallons (or liters) of purified water from the local supermarket for making fresh sea water and replacing evaporation can be considered a manageable practice. Note that over the long term, purifying water at home with a reverse osmosis or deionization system is far more cost effective than buying water at a store. Compare purifying your own water for roughly $0.05 per gallon (2.2 l) to buying water at a cost of $0.50 (or more) for the same volume, and it becomes clear that a purification unit can pay for itself over a relatively short period of time. Additionally, many of these systems produce water of far greater purity than that available at supermarkets, further extending the hobbyist's control over water parameters.

It is important to utilize a salt mix that provides the closest approximation of natural sea water possible. Certain aspects of the mix, such as the concentrations of calcium and magnesium and the alkalinity, will change with time as a result of the rates of removal by aquarium livestock.

The effort should be made to choose a salt mix that has the closest possible profile to that of natural sea water. Look for a product that states the concentrations of the elements present in the mix somewhere on the label at a seawater density of 1.024 g/cm^3, and match that with Figure 1. If the product you want to use doesn't list this information on the label, contact the manufacturer and ask for a guaranteed or average analysis on their mix. If the manufacturer refuses or cannot fulfill your request, look for another product.

In addition to providing the proper elemental concentrations, the salt should mix to a pH of 8.2–8.4 and have adequate alkalinity to maintain this pH for some time. Be leery of salt mixes that boast enhanced concentrations of elements such as calcium and magnesium; these enhancements come at the price of decreasing the concentrations of other elements from the mix, and because a nano-reef is such a small and potentially unstable system, it is recommended that you use the composition of natural sea water as the ideal model from which to base your synthetic salt choice.

pH AND ALKALINITY

pH and alkalinity refer to the relative acidity of a solution and the ability for that acidity to remain stable. The average pH of sea water is approximately 8.3; this indicates that free hydrogen ions are in lesser abundance than free hydroxide ions and is a result of the plethora of substances in sea water to which free hydrogen ions become bound. Were the concentration of hydrogen ions to increase, the pH of the water would decrease. Substances responsible for maintaining pH stability are commonly referred to as **buffers**. The sum of the concentrations of these substances yields the alkalinity.

Coralline algae, among other organisms, will benefit from regular additions of a buffering agent.

Changes in the pH of natural sea water of more than a few tenths of a unit occur very little over a short period of time, meaning that captive livestock will react poorly to such occurrences in an aquarium. Therefore, it is in the best interest of the hobbyist to make every effort to establish and maintain proper pH and alkalinity in a nano-reef. Due to the small volume of water and associated difficulty in controlling the reactions taking place, the use of pH-adjusting products in a nano-reef should be avoided if at all possible. This is a key reason that the use of a premium salt mix that establishes these levels automatically is so important.

Regular addition of a buffer of some sort will be required to maintain the pH within a narrow range. The continuous use of an electronic pH meter can benefit the hobbyist in two ways: It constantly reads the pH of the water, and it indicates the range that the pH travels on a daily basis. The greater this range, the lower the alkalinity tends to be.

By monitoring the range that the pH travels, a hobbyist can determine when it is time to formally test the water for alkalinity and add a buffering supplement. Maintaining the alkalinity at 8 dKH (3.0 meq/L) is usually adequate to keep pH within the recommended range.

The Backbone of a Nano-Reef

The elements and substances that contribute directly to the growth of reef-building organisms and chemical stability of the water are of great importance to reef aquaria. Calcium, magnesium, strontium, iodine, trace elements, and carbonate and bicarbonate ions are incorporated into the skeletal and tissue mass of aquatic organisms, and their concentrations gradually diminish with time. It is important to consider each of these elements and ions individually and then gain an understanding of how they work together. All reef hobbyists should take the time to become proficient in this area, but to those maintaining nano-reefs it is of *particular* importance, because they have to exercise much greater control over the water chemistry in their aquaria.

CALCIUM

Calcium is one of the major elements, with an average concentration of approximately 412 ppm. It is the third most abundant **cation** in sea water and is utilized by many marine organisms as a component of skeletal mass. Reef-building organisms secrete layers of **aragonite**, a form of calcium carbonate, to create additional mass; hence, the reef is able to grow and recover from damage incurred during storms and from the feeding activities of various fishes and invertebrates. Calcium makes up approximately 38–39% of aragonite by weight.

Large-polyp stony corals, such as the Lobophyllia *sp. shown, may be kept in nano-reef aquaria by advanced hobbyists, but keep in mind that the care requirements for these corals and their close allies are often hard to meet in nano-reef systems.*

Because calcium must be maintained above a minimum concentration for noticeable growth of coralline algae, corals, clams, etc., it must be tested for on a regular basis and supplemented as needed. There are many types of calcium supplements available to reef hobbyists. However, the nano-reef hobbyist has limited choices to work with. The reason

Propagation of corals, such as through making cuttings from a large colony, enable a hobbyist to quickly and often inexpensively diversify the livestock in nano-reef aquaria and help reduce the demand for wild-collected corals, if ever so slightly.

for this is that certain calcium supplements may impact the water chemistry in undesirable ways that complicate the maintenance of such a small aquarium.

Kalkwasser, or calcium hydroxide, is a salt that dissociates into calcium and hydroxide ions. Though it has the benefit of being approximately 51% calcium by dry weight, a saturated kalkwasser solution has a pH of approximately 12.5, making it a poor choice of calcium supplementation in a nano-reef owing to the danger of killing all livestock by making even the smallest error in dosing. This is a calcium supplement suited to larger aquaria.

Chelated calcium, such as calcium-EDTA (ethylenedi-aminetetraacetic acid) and calcium gluconate, is composed of calcium ions bound to a large organic molecule. Approximately 9–12% of the total weight of chelated calcium is attributable to the calcium itself; the rest (approximately 88–91%) is organic material. While this type of supplement has no direct effect on the pH or alkalinity of the water, its use can rapidly cause water quality to deteriorate as dissolved organic material accrues. A product of the deterioration of organic material is phosphate, which will encourage the growth of algae and cyanobacteria under the proper conditions. In a well-stocked nano-reef, the calcium demand may be great enough to warrant calcium dosing on a daily basis, and the more chelated calcium added to the system, the greater the amount of organic material entering it. In light of these facts, it becomes apparent that this sort of calcium supplement is not suited to nano-reef aquaria.

A beautiful coral reef. Scenes such as this one are largely responsible for the interest in the marine aquarium hobby.

Calcium chloride is a salt that readily dissociates into calcium and chloride ions. Calcium accounts for approximately 35% dry weight of this salt. A saturated solution of calcium chloride has a pH of approximately 9.5 and will not impact the pH of a reef aquarium *directly* in the same manner that kalkwasser does. If, however, the concentration of magnesium in the water is not adequate and/or too much calcium is added at once, a rapid influx of calcium ions can deplete alkalinity in the aquarium. As long as the manufacturer's directions are followed and the magnesium is within the proper range, calcium chloride salts or solutions are a good choice for use in nano-reef aquaria. The subject of chloride imbalance that is so hotly debated in forums can be disregarded by making regular partial water changes to re-establish the proper ionic ratios, approximate though they may be relative to natural sea water.

Calcium carbonate is a salt that has relatively low solubility in water. However, it can be very useful to the nano-reef hobbyist. All calcium carbonate-based supplements that are used in reef aquaria are either based on actual aragonite or else mimic aragonite's chemical build. The significance is that aragonite is the more soluble of the two forms of calcium carbonate; the other form, calcite, is not very soluble at all in sea water. Aragonite contains not only calcium but also carbonate (~59% w/v), strontium (~7% w/v), magnesium (~1% w/v), potassium (~0.5% w/v), and other minor and trace elements.

Because aragonite has low solubility in sea water, it cannot be overdosed; the dissolution of aragonite ceases once the saturation point of the water has been reached. While this may seem counterproductive to the hobbyist's efforts to control the calcium concentration in the aquarium, it actually enables calcium to gradually enter the water as corals and other reef-building organisms take up the available calcium. Even though these types of products don't contribute enough magnesium to maintain the required concentration, they have the ability to maintain calcium and alkalinity within the desired ranges when used in conjunction with accurate test kits and will not negatively impact water quality or alter pH in the process. These products are perhaps the best choice of calcium supplementation for nano-reef aquaria.

MAGNESIUM

Magnesium is the second most prevalent cation in sea water, present at an average concentration of

A Nano-Note on Magnesium

The presence of adequate magnesium (~1,288 ppm) in a marine aquarium helps prevent calcium from bonding with carbonates; in this event, the newly formed calcium carbonate is insoluble, and not only depletes the carbonate concentration (lowering alkalinity), but it wastes calcium. It's suggested that you measure the magnesium concentration in the aquarium with a good test kit, then use a magnesium supplement to correct the deficiency.

approximately 1,288 ppm. As mentioned earlier, magnesium is a component of aragonite, which indicates that magnesium has importance to reef-building organisms. However, another major role that magnesium plays involves maintaining the calcium/carbonate balance in sea water.

In the absence of adequate magnesium, calcium ions bond freely with carbonate ions, creating a relatively insoluble salt that falls out of solution to the bottom (of the aquarium in this case). This reaction is visible to the unaided eye, appearing like a snowstorm in the water. Hobbyists who have a relatively difficult time maintaining the calcium concentration in their aquaria within the desired range, regardless of how much calcium they supplement, are "victims" of this scenario. These same hobbyists often find that alkalinity is difficult to maintain in their aquaria. The problem is easily solved by supplementing magnesium to attain a concentration of at least 1,288 ppm. In doing so, less tinkering is required to maintain proper calcium and alkalinity in a nano-reef, tinkering which could otherwise cause wild fluctuations in the aquarium.

Magnesium is an expensive component of synthetic salt mixes, so inexpensive mixes are often magnesium deficient. You can look at this two ways: You could purchase an inexpensive salt now to save some money and

Magnesium additions are important to corals both directly and indirectly, as a low magnesium level may cause problems in maintaining a balanced calcium level.

The Nano-Reef System

23

PART ONE

then be forced to supplement magnesium when problems with calcium and alkalinity begin to occur, or you could purchase a high-quality mix from day one and continue to use it throughout the duration of nano-reef maintenance. In the long run, you might actually *save* money by using a premium salt mix, as wasted calcium and alkalinity supplements are a result of magnesium deficiency.

Magnesium supplements are typically prepared with some form of magnesium chloride and/or magnesium sulfate. As with any chemical supplement, it is important to determine the concentration in the aquarium *before* dosing; blindly adding a product to an aquarium has unpredictable results and generally wastes the product and therefore your money.

STRONTIUM

Strontium is in the same group of elements as calcium and magnesium, which may account for its uptake by various aquatic organisms as a component of skeletal material. Although it has been labeled as a toxin to these organisms from time to time, it is quite reasonable to assume that at

Strontium is thought by many hobbyists to reduce the tendency for coral tissue to pull away from the skeleton. There is evidence to support that strontium ions actually form the nucleus for aragonite, the mineral that coral skeletal material is composed of. Regardless of whether one or the other is true, strontium is observed to follow a type of depletion in marine waters, indicating that it's used by marine life. It is an important element in marine aquaria and should be dosed as required.

natural seawater concentrations, it poses no harm to them. Additionally, the use of strontium in reef aquaria has shown evidence of enabling coral tissue to adhere to the skeleton more readily. So little strontium is required (the natural seawater concentration is slightly less than 8 ppm) that it often makes no sense to court danger. The use of a strontium- or aragonite-based supplement will supply an adequate concentration of this element for the nano-reef.

IODINE

Iodine is a minor element and the first non-metal that has been discussed so far. In sea water, iodine exists primarily in two forms: iodide and iodate. In spite of the fact that the sum of all iodine species in natural sea water is quite low (approximately 0.06 ppm on average), this element is very important to fishes, crustaceans, many photosynthetic organisms including macroalgae, and **hermatypic organisms**. An in-depth discussion of iodine interaction with these organisms is beyond the scope of this book; however, a brief description of the importance of iodine to the hermatypic organisms referred to a moment ago follows below.

Under intense illumination and in the presence of adequate concentrations of nutrients and a carbon source, zooxanthellae carry out the process of photosynthesis, producing simple sugars (and other organic material) as well as oxygen gas. This is a highly simplified description of the process, but for the sake of this example it will suffice. The host organism utilizes the sugar as a source of energy and may derive all the food it needs in this

> **Hermatypic Organisms**
> Hermatypic organisms are those that house symbiotic algae (zooxanthellae) in their tissues for the production of food. They rely on light of the proper intensity and spectral characteristics to provide the algae with the energy they need to carry out photosynthesis.

fashion, not having to rely upon the capture of plankton to supplement its dietary requirements. The oxygen, however, is a source of irritation to the sensitive soft tissues of the host organism and must be expelled or detoxified in some manner. Iodide facilitates this detoxification by bonding with the free oxygen molecule and forming iodate, which does not irritate the tissues. For this reason alone, iodine supplementation is warranted in all reef aquaria.

As their name suggests, trace elements are present in minute quantities in sea water. Many trace elements are, however, involved with specific biological reactions and are therefore vitally important to the continued health and survival of marine organisms.

While the other elements that have been discussed up to this point may be slightly overdosed with no cause for unnecessary concern, this is not the case with iodine. The concentration should be monitored with regular testing and adjusted to a concentration of 0.05–0.08 ppm—no more. Excessive concentrations of iodine can kill beneficial bacteria in aquatic systems, as well as irritate and destroy sensitive tissue in extreme overdoses. Because the desired concentration is so small, iodine supplementation in the confines of a nano-reef must be done very carefully.

Though many manufacturers produce liquid iodine supplements, there are three basic categories that the supplements fall under: those that contain iodide, those that contain iodide and chelated iodine, and those that contain iodide and elemental iodine. The two former types of supplements are usually quite dilute yet still effective, and therefore the safest choice for use in a nano-reef.

Solutions containing iodide and elemental iodine, such as the various brands of Lugol's Solution on the market, are not suited for use in nano-reefs owing to their strength; such products can overdose a nano-reef with one drop of undiluted solution. Supplements of this type are suitable for use in larger reef systems.

TRACE ELEMENTS

Trace elements constitute less than 0.0005% of the total dissolved substances in sea water by weight. Of the 77 or so naturally occurring elements that scientists have been able to detect in sea water, 52 of them are trace elements, 31 of which exhibit non-conservative behavior. Of these, at least 13 appear to be nutrients (see Figure 1.3a) expressly required for the growth of primary

producers such as algae, and many others are either incorporated into living tissue or skeletal material or undergo chemical interactions that cause their depletion in surface waters (see Figure 1.3b).

Non-conservative trace elements are very important to aquatic organisms, for many are utilized in enzymatic reactions, including photosynthesis and the metabolism of protein. Unless you have access to an atomic emission spectrometer or highly sensitive and specialized analytical chemistry testing equipment, you can forget about measuring the concentrations of the trace elements present in your aquarium. Because the concentrations of these elements are so minute, the most reliable way to control them is to use a premium salt mix that yields an accurate representation of natural sea water, and to perform frequent partial water changes. Commercially available trace element supplements may not present these non-conservative elements in the proper concentrations. However, one need not be fastidious about trace element addition in a

Figure 1.3a. Trace Elements Exhibiting Nutrient-Type Behavior

Beryllium	Arsenic
Phosphorus	Selenium
Chromium	Silver
Nickel	Cadmium
Copper	Iodine
Zinc	Barium
Germanium	

Figure 1.3b. Trace Elements Exhibiting Surface Depletion

Scandium	Gadolinium
Vanadium	Terbium
Iron	Dysprosium
Cobalt	Holmium
Lanthanum	Erbium
Cerium	Thulium
Praseodymium	Ytterbium
Neodymium	Lutetium
Samarium	
Europium	

The Nano-Reef System

27

PART ONE

marine aquarium as long as the product is not overdosed. In other words, trace element supplements are fine for use in a nano-reef.

Like iodine, other trace elements are bound by latent organic material in water, leading to their rapid removal by protein skimmers (which remove organic material and collect it in a waste receptacle). Additionally, activated carbon will remove trace elements from water long after it has reached its capacity for removing organic material. If your intention is to rely upon a powerful protein skimmer and/or activated carbon filtration, increasing the daily dosage of a trace element supplement may be called for. The best way to use trace element supplements is to begin by using $1/2$ of the manufacturer's recommended dosage and then gradually increasing the dose over time if the livestock appears to be gaining some benefit. If more than one trace element supplement is used on the same system, then you will need to cut the dosage accordingly ($1/4$ the recommended dose of each if using two, and so on).

Minimizing Failure

One of the most important factors in achieving success with a nano-reef is to never allow the concentrations of nutrients to get out of hand. The decomposition of latent organic material (such as from animal waste and overfeeding) leads to problems with phosphate and ammonia, and unfiltered tap water and low-grade salt mixes and supplements may contain silica. In a large aquarium, these nutrients are diluted into the water, and their impact on a system is temporarily delayed, at least until the concentrations reach the levels required for unwanted organisms to flourish. In contrast, these substances accumulate much more rapidly in a nano-reef, making it imperative to pay close attention to water quality and avoid the temptation to overfeed.

Hobbyists interested in nano-reef aquaria should already be familiar with the nitrogen cycle, so it won't be detailed here other than to summarize it as follows. Ammonia is oxidized by a group of bacteria, the end result being nitrite; the nitrite, in turn, is oxidized by another group of bacteria to

Utilizing Efficient Protein Skimming and/or Chemical Filtration

Protein skimming will be discussed in detail in a following section. For now, it should be mentioned that a good protein skimmer is worth its weight in gold for any marine aquarium hobbyist (but particularly for the nano-reef hobbyist). By physically removing all forms of latent organic material from the water, a protein skimmer is an indispensable part of any successful marine aquarium filtration system. In a nano-reef, where the amount of this material can quickly get out of hand, a protein skimmer can save the lives of livestock and maintain a system's healthy appearance.

Nano-Note
Nitrite is *slightly* less toxic to aquatic organisms than unionized ammonia. It becomes dangerous to fish as the concentration approaches 0.50 ppm.

form nitrate. The last step in the cycle is the reduction of nitrate to nitrogen and oxygen gas. This description is very simplified, for there are additional products of the reactions; however this description will suffice for the purpose of this discussion.

AMMONIA (NH3)

Ammonia is a nitrogen-bearing molecule that is created as animals metabolize organic material. It interferes with oxygen transport in the blood and is therefore toxic to aquatic organisms, becoming potentially deadly to fish whenever the concentration exceeds 0.02 ppm. The temperature and pH of the water influence the percentage of total ammonia that exists in the toxic, unionized form of NH3; the remaining ammonia exists as ionized ammonium (NH_4^+), which does not affect animals in the same manner as ammonia. Ammonium is an ion, not a gas like ammonia, and does not pass through fishes' gills[1]. Unfortunately, high-pH, high-temperature environments, such as those found in the typical marine aquarium, correspond to an unionized ammonia percentage in excess of safe levels. For example, at a pH of 8.3 and a temperature of 79°F (26°C), approximately 11% of the total ammonia will be toxic. This means that in order to remain within the aforementioned "safe" ammonia concentration, the total ammonia in the system cannot exceed 0.18 ppm.

NITRITE (NO2) AND NITRATE (NO3)

As mentioned earlier, nitrate is produced by the oxidation of nitrite. Because the concentration of nitrate in natural sea

The concentration of ammonia in marine aquaria, as in all aquaria, should be immeasurable.

Feeding Livestock Sensibly

It might seem elementary that you should feed the proper foods to the livestock in your nano-reef. However, given the scope of foods available to hobbyists at the present time, a correct decision can be difficult, leading often to unsuccessful experimentation and uneaten food (and wasted money). Nano-reef aquarists should utilize simple foods, such as live brine shrimp, live or preserved zooplankton, and plant material such

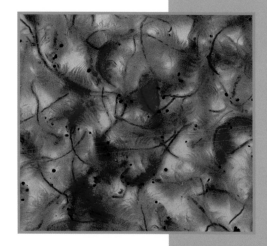

as nori. You may choose to fortify these foods with vitamin supplements to increase their benefit to livestock, but it is strongly advised that the use of supplements containing highly unsaturated omega-3 and -6 fatty acids not be used, as these can *rapidly* degrade water quality in a nano-reef. Prepared foods, such as pellets, are fine to feed fish as long as they are not allowed to deteriorate in filters or the crevices of live rock. Plankton suspensions should be fed in moderation in nano-reefs, but only use $1/4$ to $1/2$ of the manufacturer's recommended dosage.

Rinsing frozen food is absolutely vital in all aquaria. The reason is that the solution present in the food is full of organic material. Allowing this solution to enter the aquarium will directly decrease water quality through the introduction of the dissolved organic matter (DOM), none of which benefit the livestock. Therefore, rinse the frozen food under running tap water until it is thawed, and then add the food particles to the aquarium. Using this approach, phosphate problems often clear up in a matter of weeks using no additional means of filtration other than that already existing on the system in question.

Once the livestock are full, they will cease to feed, and any leftovers will float aimlessly around the aquarium until they settle in some hidden location or wind up in a filter intake. In both cases, bacterial degradation of food will decrease water quality. The best use of food is when the livestock eats all of it, and the only way to accomplish this is to learn through experience how much the animals will eat before they have reached their fill, and then not exceed this amount of feeding at any time.

water may be extremely low (almost immeasurable) over reefs, it is wise to replicate this characteristic in reef aquaria. However, it has generally been noted that a nitrate concentration of up to 20 ppm will be tolerated by many reef invertebrates, so this should be considered the upper limit of safety[2].

The goal of every aquarium hobbyist should be to maintain the total ammonia and nitrite concentrations as close to 0 ppm (or immeasurable) as possible. This is accomplished through sensible feeding, limiting the use of supplements with organic components, ensuring that the biological filter has been sufficiently matured *prior* to adding ornamental livestock, and resisting the temptation to overstock the aquarium. In any reef aquarium, nitrate should not be allowed to exceed a concentration of 20 ppm; the closer to 0 ppm this concentration, the better. Utilizing porous live rock and/or a nitrate-removing medium or filtration system, and regular, frequent water changes with purified water and a premium synthetic sea salt mix will enable a hobbyist to attain this goal in a nano-reef.

PHOSPHATE (PO4)

Phosphate is a constituent of latent **organic material**. As alluded to earlier, excessive phosphate opens the door to proliferation of cyanobacteria and filamentous algae, and therefore its concentration should be minimized in any aquarium. The obvious means of doing so is to minimize the amount of decaying organic material in the system.

Organic material exists in two forms: particulate and dissolved. Particulate organic material (POM) is comprised largely of uneaten food (which may include the

The many forms of Xenia *available to hobbyists often flourish in nano-reef aquaria due to their relatively low requirements. It has been suggested by some that the presence of phosphate in the water encourages the growth and proliferation of* Xenia *sp., but phosphate should not be encouraged to accumulate in nano-reef aquaria because of the associated negative impact in water quality that accompanies it. Additionally, many nano-reef owners discover, often to their dismay, that* Xenia *sp. can quickly "take over" a small aquarium and damage corals in the process.*

Increasing the probability of success with your nano-reef starts with a solid understanding of the importance of good water quality. If you can control the water quality then you're 90 percent of the way there.

various types of frozen and prepared fish food as well as invertebrate foods such as algae and plankton suspensions), deceased livestock, and decaying tissue (whether it be from plant or animal). It is consumed and transformed by livestock and bacteria to create additional particulate organic material as well as dissolved organic material.

Dissolved organic material (DOM) exists as high-molecular-weight molecules and is exemplified by such substances as gluconate and EDTA (both used to chelate various elements in some liquid supplements) and the less complex products of particulate organic material degradation. DOM is less complex in structure and is therefore easily utilized by the nuisance organisms referred to moments ago.

Phosphate comes into play because it is a component of cellular tissue; without it, the growth of living organisms is not possible. Whereas most advanced organisms obtain phosphate through the digestion of food, simple organisms require that the phosphate be made available in a less complex form (which is provided by the degradation of POM and DOM). Therefore, the best way to control the concentrations of both phosphate and DOM is to limit the amount of POM in the aquarium. This is of particular importance in a nano-reef, because allowing the concentration of latent organic material to reach a concentration at which nuisance organisms begin to thrive can be difficult to correct.

The methods used to minimize the tendency for this problem to develop are as simple as feeding the livestock sensibly, utilizing efficient protein skimming and/or chemical filtration, and performing regular

Many nano-reef systems have a variety of different organisms in them. Be sure to add only what is needed for them, and try not to guess what they may need based on assumptions.

partial water changes. Water changes have already been discussed, but the other points can be addressed individually.

A sensible approach to feeding is probably more complicated than it initially seems. You must choose foods that your livestock will eat, rinse frozen foods in a fine mesh net with running water *prior* to placing them in the aquarium, and avoid the temptation to overfeed no matter how hungry the fish may look.

SILICA

Silica is the term given to molecules that contain the element silicon. As has been seen in the discussion of nutrients, the presence of silica in a marine aquarium encourages the growth and proliferation of diatoms. While these organisms essentially have no direct impact on the livestock, they detract from the appearance of the aquarium. Controlling their population is as simple as eliminating the introduction of silica to the

Silica enters marine aquaria through unpurified tap water and through certain types of chemical supplements. Some amount of silica may be present in most marine aquaria as a matter of unintended additions, and this is fine. While the presence of excessive silica will not seriously impact water quality, it will encourage the growth and reproduction of diatoms, silica-based dinoflagellates that appear as a fine brown dust that detracts from the general appearance of an aquarium. The use of purified water is the first step in avoiding this problem, and you might might need to clean the tank by hand sometimes.

nano-reef, which in itself is comprised of nothing more than the use of purified water and a high-quality synthetic salt mix. Should diatoms become a problem, determine the source of silica and eliminate it; having done so, the diatoms will begin to die on their own. If you prefer to act more aggressively on the matter, there are chemical filtration media available that will remove silica from marine aquaria. The limitation of these media lies in whether or not space exists in the nano-reef to employ them.

Final Thoughts on Chemical Stability in the Nano-Reef

The topic of chemical stability has been mentioned numerous times throughout this chapter. One means to accomplish relatively steady concentrations of important elements in an aquarium is to add supplements daily at $1/7$ the manufacturer's weekly recommended dosage. If one were to add supplements on one day of the week only (for instance, Saturday), the concentrations of elements in the aquarium would spike and then gradually fall until the following week arrived, whereupon the cycle would be repeated. This is completely unnatural to the livestock and could cause undesirable chemical reactions, particularly when the aquarium is as small as a nano-reef. To exercise even greater stability, a hobbyist can obtain one or more drip-dosing devices, determine the rate of daily evaporation from the aquarium, add the proper volumes of supplements, and maintain stable salinity and concentrations of non-conservative elements simultaneously. This is the ultimate level of care for a nano-reef.

Many of the supplements available to hobbyists are comprised of salts with chloride components. As noted in the section discussing calcium chloride, the concern of attaining a so-called "chloride imbalance" in a nano-reef is relaxed by

Concentration Concerns

If the concentration of one or more elements in a nano-reef is found to be deficient, it is imperative that changes be made gradually rather than all at once. This is particularly true of large discrepancies in the desired concentrations, because dosing at a rate that rapidly brings about change is very likely to impact the livestock in a negative fashion.

The Nano-Reef System

35

PART ONE

Colonial polyps, such as the star polyps shown here, will colonize new surfaces relatively quickly if conditions are conducive, and therefore are favored by many nano-reef hobbyists.

doing nothing more than performing regular partial water changes, re-establishing the proper approximate ionic ratios in the water. Performing a 20% water change every week may entail preparing no more than 1 gallon (2.2 l) of sea water in some cases, and this is a small price to pay for the benefit of keeping the water quality within the desired ranges of respective concentrations.

INCREASING THE PROBABILITY FOR SUCCESS WITH A NANO-REEF AQUARIUM

The long-term maintenance of any aquarium depends on a sensible approach to husbandry. If one can control the water quality, one is 90% of the way to becoming a successful nano-reef hobbyist. The following is a brief discussion of the methods used to accomplish this goal.

• **Use purified water.** Tap water is full of substances that can negatively impact aquarium livestock and the overall appearance of the aquarium. Among these substances are chlorine, chloramines, ammonia, nitrate, phosphate, silicate, and heavy metals. Calcium, magnesium, sodium, potassium, chloride, and sulfate are also present, and while these may not be detrimental to the livestock, their concentrations are unknown and unreliable for the reef hobbyist. These substances are often added to bottled water to improve its palatability. However, the problem again is that without formal testing, there is no way to know exactly what is in the water. Do not let that fact dissuade you from using store-bought purified water— just keep it in mind. As has been mentioned, water purified at home not only removes up to 99.9% of dissolved and particulate impurities, but it is also about $1/10$ the cost per gallon (2.2 l) of store-bought water. In any case, the importance of starting with a "clean slate" (i.e., purified water) cannot be understated.

- **Regularly test the aquarium water.** Without testing the water on a regular basis, there is no way to know which parameters are out of range and how to correct the problem. Do yourself a favor: Purchase a set of accurate test kits and replace the reagents at least once a year (their accuracy deteriorates with time), regardless of what they cost. You will be amazed at the difference in readings between a good test kit and one marketed for only a few dollars. The few extra dollars spent in purchasing accurate test kits will be repaid in the hundreds or thousands of dollars saved in replacing deceased livestock that resulted from an inaccurate reading from an inexpensive, low-grade kit.

Performing regular partial water changes on your nano-reef system will help keep it balanced and healthy for a long time.

- **Perform regular partial water changes.** In a small aquarium, the ionic balance of the water is easily altered by the relatively high stocking density of livestock and the difficulty of properly dosing necessary supplements. Therefore, replacing a percentage of the water in the aquarium with sea water of the proper ionic ratios on a regular basis is the nano-reef hobbyist's most effective means of maintaining stable water parameters.

- **Use supplements wisely.** Hobbyists tend to overuse supplements, either as a result of their failure to test water and determine how much of a supplement actually *needs* to be added, or because they think that adding more of a supplement will get better results than going by the manufacturer's recommended dosage. In either case, avoid the temptation to overuse supplements, particularly in a nano-reef. Remember the opening discussion to this book regarding the difficulty of maintaining stable parameters in small volumes of water and take that information to heart when popping the top on a supplement. Read the label completely before using the product, know the concentration of the parameter in your aquarium if at all possible, refrain from exceeding the recommended dosage, and continue dosing only long enough to attain the desired concentration. This approach will save you money and frustration in the long run.

- **Avoid overfeeding.** This topic has already been discussed in detail. Overfeeding is a quick means of failure in any aquarium, but in a nano-reef it should be avoided at all costs.

Chapter Two

Components of a Nano-Reef

Because it is highly unlikely that you'll want to make equipment changes to your nano-reef after you've initially set it up, it is important to do it properly the first time. Attention must be paid to the quality of components available to you and how they will lend themselves to use in a nano-reef. For instance, there are numerous high-end protein skimmers that are capable of extracting practically all of the organic material from a small aquarium. However, most require a sump to operate in or on, which in either case is outside the scope of the nano-reef setup. That being said, it becomes very important to make decisions and purchases of equipment for your nano-reef wisely.

Selecting an Aquarium

The first step of setting up a nano-reef is, as you might expect, selecting an aquarium. There are numerous sizes and shapes of aquaria available to hobbyists that are suitable for use as a nano-reef; rectangles, cubes, hexagons, and bow-faced tanks with rounded, squared, and beveled edges (flat-backed hexagons) are available in glass and acrylic construction. The determining factors behind aquarium selection are typically the space available for placement and the hobbyist's finances.

It is recommended that you purchase the largest nano-reef your space and finances can manage. This may mean using a tank of 2 gallons (4.4 l) or less in volume, and if so, fine; systems this

A flourishing nano-reef, such as this one, will need a high level of dissolved oxygen to continue to thrive. Water movement and circulation are key here and should not be overlooked.

small have been successfully maintained for years, though it is preferable to make use of tanks in the 5- to 7-gallon range (11 to 15.5 l) whenever space permits.

One of the main risks of maintaining a small volume of water where water pumps and intense lighting are used is that the concentration of dissolved oxygen can be limited as a function of water temperature. This being the case, look for aquaria with the maximum amount of surface area possible to help increase gas exchange at the surface; the greater the surface area, the better the gas exchange, and the healthier the livestock will remain.

In terms of weight, the decision of whether to purchase a glass or acrylic aquarium is less important with small systems such as a nano-reef than it is when setting up larger aquaria. For example, the difference in weight between a 10-gallon (22-l) glass aquarium and one made of acrylic is relatively small and is unlikely to significantly impact the stability of a proper aquarium stand or cabinet. Clarity of the material used is one consideration; acrylic is crystal clear, whereas regular glass has a very slight green tint. The extent to which this tinting alters the perceived appearance of the livestock is probably so slight as to be negligible. Additionally, some manufacturers may offer nano-reef aquaria constructed of colorless glass, negating this advantage of acrylic. The real determining factor behind construction is price. Acrylic aquaria are nearly always more expensive than glass aquaria of the same shape and volume. Nano-reefs have been maintained in both glass and acrylic aquaria, and there is no obvious difference in performance that makes one far better than the other.

Cabinet Selection

One of the advantages of setting up a nano-reef is that the piece of furniture that the aquarium sits on doesn't have to be specifically built for the express purpose of holding an aquarium. Virtually any sturdy table, desk, cabinet, or similar item may be used, as long as it can handle the weight of the full system when it is up and running. Consideration should be given to the fact that water from the aquarium may spill, leak, drip, or spray from time to time during the course of normal operation, and that certain materials will not react well to exposure to salt water. Metal filing cabinets come instantly to mind, as do tables or desks made of laminated fiber board. The former will rust (unless treated with an anti-rusting paint), and the latter may bubble and disintegrate. Wood that is exposed to saltwater spray or salt creep may damage the finish or the wood itself.

To help minimize water damage to surfaces nearby, you might consider placing the aquarium into a shallow plastic pan for an added measure of security. If you are very careful, this precautionary step may be avoided, but know that in nearly all cases, when an aquarium is placed upon a wood surface, it will leave a watermark or a footprint that may never come off—unless the surface is refinished, of course. Before you make a final decision regarding a

Choosing the proper cabinet to place your nano-reef on is extremely important. Also, don't forget to make sure it sits level before filling the tank with water.

stand, refer to the aquarium manufacturer's warranty information and be sure that you abide by its stipulations for situating the tank, should any exist. Some of the complete nano-reef packages that are now available include a stand of sorts, and if these items appeal to you, then by all means purchase one with your setup.

Filtration

The means of maintaining adequate water quality are accomplished by efficient mechanical, biological, and chemical filtration. One way or another, each of these filtration aspects generally plays a role in successful aquarium husbandry, and each is no different in the nano-reef than any other aquarium setup.

MECHANICAL FILTRATION

This type of filtration physically removes particulate material from the water. The particulate material may include detritus and pieces of uneaten food. Mechanical filtration is commonly accomplished by passing aquarium water through a type of foam or floss. As the water passes through, large particles are strained out. Eventually, the hobbyist must remove the mechanical filter and rinse it (preferably in a bucket of "old" sea water from performing a water change), then place it back in the proper location to resume operation.

Mechanical filtration is often considered the first step of filtering water because it traps particles and enables their removal before bacteria have a chance to fully decompose them, which leads to better overall water quality in the end. Regularly checking and cleaning the mechanical filtration media will minimize the likelihood that organic material is given a sufficient chance to break down. These checks are even more highly recommended in a nano-reef since you'll be dealing with a generally smaller volume of water compared to other aquariums.

Features to look for in mechanical filtration media are long-term durability and a pore size that enables water to pass easily, but which is still small enough to trap relatively small particles of organic material. Plastic foam or sponge is probably the best

Some hobbyists may choose to rely on a canister filter, such as the items shown, to perform filtration on their nano-reef. The author typically employs an effective protein skimmer and live rock to perform the majority of filtration duties in nano-reef aquaria, using canister filters on an intermittent basis if activated carbon or some other chemical filtration media are required.

in this aspect. Ceramic rings or noodles may enable particles to pass too easily, and some hobbyists report that they are not as effective as foam. Filter floss tends to plug too readily and forces water around the outside of the filter, where the depth of the floss is least; like ceramic media, it just doesn't perform as well as reticulated foam. The great thing about this medium is that it can be squeezed out and rinsed in a bucket of sea water and re-used time and time again. By contrast, filter floss must be discarded and replaced frequently. Foam and filter floss are also inexpensive when compared to ceramic mechanical filtration media—something else the aquarist on a budget should consider.

Live rock is probably the best biological filtration material that is available for use in marine systems of all types.

BIOLOGICAL FILTRATION

Biological filtration is performed by living organisms and generally refers to the nitrogen and phosphate cycles carried out by bacteria, plants, and cyanobacteria. Without biological filtration in an aquarium, the concentration of ammonia would rise steadily and no marine organisms could survive. The goal of every hobbyist is to establish so-called **"balanced" biological filtration** in his or her aquarium; in a large sense, this means that the rates of ammonia and nitrite oxidation equal the rates of their production, with the end result being immeasurable concentrations of both. In order for balanced biological filtration to exist, certain criteria must be met.

- First, sufficient surface area must exist for the colonization of beneficial bacteria or cyanobacteria (slime algae). These organisms attach themselves to surfaces, so the greater the surface area available to them, the higher their population density can be, and therefore the greater the filtration potential.
- Second, the colonized area must be exposed to the proper conditions. For nitrification, bacteria require plenty of oxygen, so keeping them exposed to well-oxygenated water encourages rapid and efficient processing of ammonia and nitrite. Conversely, for nitrate reduction, *absence* of oxygen is required, as is darkness.
- Third, the rate of nutrient input to the aquarium must not exceed the rate of nutrient uptake (i.e., don't overfeed).

Live sand comes in many sizes. Pictured is a coarser type, which is usually used in biotope-specific aquariums.

- Fourth, these beneficial organisms must not be continuously molested, which would interfere with their ability to take in nutrients.
- Fifth, the organisms must not compete with each other for nutrients to the extent that a large-scale population crash results. This situation can occur when a source of nutrients is continuously added to the aquarium, forcing the population of nitrifying bacteria and/or algae to increase, then suddenly halting the nutrient input and causing wide-scale starvation.

One of the key aspects to successfully maintaining any aquarium is to limit the input of organic matter, and in the nano-reef this practice is paramount. The bottom line is that liquid or powdered invertebrate foods and plankton suspensions should be used sparingly, if at all.

It could be said that live rock and live sand are a nano-reef hobbyist's best friend. When used, enough biological filtration may exist within them so as to reduce the need for additional biological filtration media. A few nice pieces of premium live rock and a $^1/_2$-inch (2.5-cm) layer of live sand not only look natural in the nano-reef, but they don't require electricity to function. To get the most for your money, look for low-density live rock, such as that which originates from a Pacific coral reef, to aquascape your nano-reef. It will displace less water than rock of greater density, and fewer pounds (kilograms) will be required to obtain the desired aquascaped appearance.

As for the live sand, you should consider the types of organisms that you intend to house in the aquarium and their habits when choosing average particle size (if you decide to use any sand at all). There are so many choices for quality aragonite sand in the aquarium market that all manners of taste can be accommodated. Keep the depth to no more than $1/2$ of an inch (2.5 cm) for two key reasons. First, the aquarium has limited volume, and every pound of sand added will displace precious water. Second, the aquarium has limited depth, and though it might not seem like much, placing an inch or more of sand (5 cm or more) on the bottom of a small aquarium can dramatically alter the system's appearance, making it look smaller than it really is.

If you're on a very tight budget and can't afford to aquascape the aquarium with live rock and sand, biological filtration must be performed by a powered unit designed for the purpose. Filters suited to nano-reef aquaria that promote biological filtration abound and are relatively inexpensive. Box filters that hang on the back of the tank, as well as canister filters, may be outfitted with media that are suited for bacterial colonization. Alternately, fluidized bed filters that keep colonized particulate media in suspension and exposed to aquarium water are very effective on small systems such as nano-reefs. When making a selection for this and any other filter, take into account the total space the filter will occupy on the back of the aquarium, because this space is limited. It is frustrating to purchase a powerful hang-on aquarium filter and then discover that it is so wide that no other equipment can be used in the same fashion. Most biological filters likely to be used with nano-reef

A Mini-Tip on Macroalgae

Although fast-growing species of macroalgae are often used to help rid the aquarium of nutrients, I advise against their dense cultivation for this purpose in small aquaria. When the algae are placed directly into the main aquarium, they follow normal light cycles, meaning that they produce oxygen and consume inorganic carbon (such as carbon dioxide) when properly illuminated, and respire oxygen and produce carbon dioxide when the lights are off. This causes the pH in the water to go through a daily cycle, with the lowest values occurring several hours after the lights have been turned off and the highest values several hours after illumination has commenced. Even in large aquaria with plenty of water and the proper alkalinity, it is not uncommon for the pH to swing between values of 8.0 at night and 8.5 during the day. In small aquaria housing a dense population of fast-growing algae, this swing can be even more pronounced. For this reason, the only manner in which I recommend the use of these algae to rid a nano-reef of nutrients is if they're housed in a refugium with reverse-daylight illumination. This entails illuminating the algae in a separate compartment (such as that which sits directly behind the nano-reef) at night when the aquarium lights are off. Water passes slowly through the compartment via a small submersible pump, and the pH in the system remains much more stable because photosynthesis is occurring at all times.

You can readily purchase activated carbon in pre-sealed bags that make changing them out much easier.

aquaria will be capable of maintaining the concentrations of ammonia and nitrite at immeasurable concentrations, provided overfeeding is avoided.

CHEMICAL FILTRATION

The removal of unwanted substances from the water via some sort of chemical adsorptive or exchange process is referred to as chemical filtration. Activated carbon is the best example of a chemical filtration media. It utilizes pores (created by exposing the carbon to phosphoric acid or steam) to trap organic molecules and remove them from the aquarium water. There are a number of filtration media that perform similar functions using different methods; some selectively remove phosphate, while others strip the water of heavy metals. In general, the use of these media is on an "as needed" basis, because proper aquarium husbandry encourages water changes that limit the accumulation of unwanted substances in the water. The one exception to this rule, in my opinion, is protein skimming, which should be in operation every minute of the day.

PROTEIN SKIMMING

A superficial glance at a protein skimmer might give the impression that it is a mechanical or biological filter. However, this Protein Skimming isn't the case. A protein skimmer utilizes very fine bubbles mixed inside a column of rapidly flowing water to strip organic material from the aquarium. The smaller the bubbles are and the longer they interact with the aquarium water, the more effective the skimmer is at stripping organics. Because nano-reefs are generally "sumpless," they must rely on protein skimmers that hang on the back of the aquarium. Here is a piece of advice that has served thousands of aquarium hobbyists well: Don't skimp on an inexpensive protein skimmer! Buy a good one and you won't regret it.

The importance of a good protein skimmer becomes clear when you see the material it pulls out of the aquarium on a regular basis. This material is full of nutrients that deteriorate water quality and encourage the growth of cyanobacteria and assorted other undesirable organisms. Continued exposure to the ammonia and other nitrogenous molecules liberated by bacterial decomposition of this organic material progressively weakens livestock. A good protein skimmer extracts the material *before* bacteria have a chance to break it down, and therefore increases the chances of long-term success with a nano-reef.

If you cannot purchase a good protein skimmer for your nano-reef in your local market and have no access to internet-based retailers, a viable alternative is a canister filter loaded with an organic adsorption media. To gain the maximum effectiveness, look for a unit that fluidizes the media, using a gentle upward flow of aquarium water to increase exposure time with each pass. Resins of this variety are typically regenerable many times using nothing more than a table salt and tap water solution and are very effective at extracting organic material from aquaria, particularly small ones. Look for a canister filter with a clear reaction column so you can observe the color of the resin and regenerate it when necessary. (The color darkens progressively, indicating exhaustion.) One attractive feature of these filters is that, unlike protein skimmers, they will not create bubbles that can disperse throughout the aquarium (a point that many experienced hobbyists can readily appreciate).

A canister filter or other device that can house one or more types of chemical filtration media and be set up in a hurry is a worthy purchase. If for some reason the aquarium water needs to be quickly stripped of some substance and you have no makeup water prepared, a small filter loaded with the appropriate media can help avert a disaster.

FILTRATION SYNERGY: PUTTING IT ALL TOGETHER

The concept of balanced filtration can be defined as "a state in which the concentrations of ammonia, nitrite, nitrate, and phosphate are immeasurable at all times." This is the state of

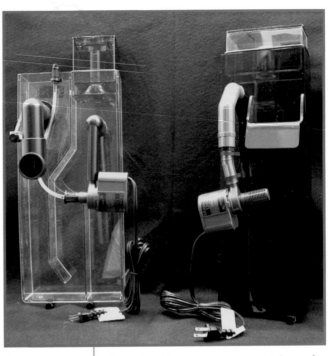

Protein skimmers are a must-have for the nano-reef enthusiast. There are many makes and models out there.

Full coverage of a nano-reef, or any reef for that matter, is beneficial because it allows the growth of light-loving organisms to flourish tank wide.

filtration that advanced reef hobbyists strive to attain in their aquaria, and it is a combination of effective mechanical, biological, and chemical filtration techniques.

Most marine aquaria, regardless of size, attain balanced filtration through the following steps:

1. Resisting the urge to add "just one more" fish or coral to an already well-stocked aquarium.
2. Performing regular water changes as outlined in the first section of this book.
3. Forcing water through a mechanical filter of some description to remove large particulate material from the aquarium, then rinsing this filter every few days to minimize the bacterial decomposition of the material.
4. Aquascaping with 1.0–1.5 lbs (2.2–3.3 kg) of premium, "low-density" live rock per gallon (3.79 l) of water volume capacity in the aquarium. The addition of 1/2 of an inch (2.5 cm) of live sand on the bottom of the aquarium increases the surface area for colonization of beneficial bacteria and further aids the rate of ammonia and nitrite oxidation.
5. Utilizing a quality protein skimmer or other means of chemical filtration to rid the aquarium of organic material.
6. Avoiding the habit of overfeeding the livestock.

Following these simple recommendations will keep water quality more stable and pollutants at a minimum, and will lead directly to healthier, more colorful livestock.

Lighting

Properly illuminating a nano-reef is no less important than it is to a larger system, for without a light source of adequate intensity and spectral composition, the organisms that rely ultimately upon photosynthesis for energy will suffer and perish. The trick is providing this lighting within the tight confines afforded by the footprint of the aquarium. Because nano-reef systems have been steadily gaining in popularity over the past few years, a few manufacturers have created specialty lighting components that create reef-friendly light without looking like an eyesore. To understand exactly what is meant by "reef-friendly" and to familiarize novice hobbyists with terms they will see when shopping for a lighting system to illuminate their nano-reef, a general overview of lighting is needed.

The vast majority of corals and their allies that are housed in reef aquaria have a symbiotic relationship with algae, called **zooxanthellae**, that reside within the tissues of the corals. Organisms hosting these algae are classified as **hermatypic** by marine biologists. Under proper illumination, the zooxanthellae begin the process of **photosynthesis**, the end result being the production of organic material that is utilized by the corals as a source of nutrients. Studies conducted by oceanographers have shown that the nutrients produced by the zooxanthellae are able to provide well over 100% of the host organism's daily requirements; in view of this, it can be generalized that hermatypic organisms rely greatly on the products of photosynthesis for survival.

This small colony of zoanthids is flourishing under intense lighting.

Even though they have polyps armed with **nematocysts** that extend to capture prey drifting by in the currents, prolonged lack of sufficient illumination usually spells demise for a hermatypic coral. Hermatypic clams, such as

The Nano-Reef System

49

PART ONE

those of the genera *Tridacna* and *Hippopus*, fare no better. The only way that these organisms can survive a lack of illumination is to have plankton and/or another food source available to them at all times while maintaining immeasurable ammonia, nitrite, and phosphate. This is impossible in even the biggest aquaria, let alone tiny systems such as nano-reefs. For this reason, providing proper lighting is essential to long-term success with hermatypic organisms.

KELVIN RATING

The **Kelvin rating**, or **Kelvin temperature**, of a light source is essentially an expression of the perceived color being emitted, regardless of the nature of the source itself (i.e., sunlight, light from an incandescent, fluorescent, or metal halide bulb, candle, or even light-emitting diode [LED]). The lower the Kelvin temperature, the redder the light appears; conversely, the higher the temperature, the bluer the light appears. Bulbs manufactured for illuminating living spaces (i.e., a dining room, etc.) are often in the 3,500–4,100 Kelvin range and produce light with a great deal of red to enhance the appearance of furnishings. Sunlight[1] at the ocean's surface, by contrast, has a temperature of approximately 6,500 Kelvin ($^+/^-$500 K, depending on the reference). With increasing depth beneath the water's surface, longer wavelengths of light are progressively refracted and absorbed by water and dissolved

This display shows the variation in color that is found in many of the most commonly used bulbs on the market.

substances, producing a deep blue appearance that you may be familiar with from watching documentaries on the world's oceans. This blue light can be replicated in an aquarium with bulbs that emit light of approximately 7,500–20,000 Kelvin, which emit light predominantly in the blue portion of the spectrum that is visible to humans. An extreme example of this blue light emission is produced by actinic bulbs; a great deal of the light they emit lies within a narrow band on the visible spectrum thought to trigger photosynthesis in zooxanthellae. (Light within this band is often called photosynthetically active radiation, or PAR.)

To the unaided human eye, visible light lies within a spectrum between red and indigo or violet. For the purposes of reef aquarium care, only light that produces the visual effect desired, and that which activates photosynthesis in the zooxanthellae, is relevant. The former is important because an aquarium is, after all, an expression of what the hobbyist feels the reef looks like. The latter is vital to the survival of hermatypic organisms. How can both be provided?

Generally speaking, hermatypic organisms will thrive when illuminated with light that falls within the range of 6,500–20,000 K. A combination of 6,500–7,100 K and actinic light produces a pleasing appearance of being near the surface of the reef, no more than 6 feet (approximately 2 meters) in depth. To produce the appearance of being deeper in the water, substitute 6,500 K lamps for those that emit light in the 10,000–20,000 K range. This approach is sensible when housing corals found only below a certain depth on the reefs.

Aquariums illuminated with 20,000K metal halides and actinics have a very distinct blue appearance to them.

INTENSITY

Kelvin temperature is one of two important physical characteristics of light, the other being **intensity**. If light of the proper wavelengths is provided, but it is not intense enough to cause photosynthesis to occur at the rate required for production of nutrients, hermatypic organisms will slowly starve.

Calculating intensity of a light source is a complex matter that extends well beyond the scope of this book. It is possible, however, to make a few operational generalizations about intensity for the purpose of this discussion:

The Nano-Reef System

51

PART ONE

There are two types of power compact fluorescent bulbs: those with square pins and those with straight pins.
A straight-pinned bulb is pictured here.

1. The closer an object is to a source of light, the greater the perceived intensity will be to that object.
2. The amount of energy consumed by a light bulb does not directly indicate the intensity of light that will be produced; in other words, "watts per gallon" (liter) really means nothing. It is the efficiency of the transfer of electricity to visible light that is important.
3. Point sources of light (such as incandescent, metal halide, and LED) appear to produce more intense light than diffuse light sources (such as fluorescent).

The intensity of light reaching hermatypic corals in the wild is in excess of that which can be reproduced artificially in the home. But as thousands of successful reef hobbyists over the past four decades will attest, it is also unnecessary. To avoid a lengthy discussion on a topic that has limited relevance to keeping a nano-reef, it is prudent to simply make some recommendations regarding intelligent choices when shopping for your nano-reef's lighting. A few years ago, hobbyists keeping tiny reef aquaria had no problem providing *intense* light; rather, the problem was that the *color* of the light was often lacking in the necessary wavelengths for continued survival of hermatypic organisms, instead favoring the growth of algae. Thankfully, there are now several compact lighting systems in the marketplace made specifically for nano-reef aquaria. These systems utilize either compact fluorescent bulbs and/or metal halide bulb(s). There are pros and cons to each approach.

POWER COMPACTS

Power compact systems consume relatively little electricity in contrast to the amount of light they emit. The bulbs heat up after being in operation for a few minutes, yet they still remain cool when compared to metal halide bulbs. As a result, they heat the water less than a halide will, a *very* important consideration. A canopy that features two to four power compact lamps (half actinic, the other half 6,500–10,000 K) of 9–18 watts each will produce enough intensity to satiate the needs of hermatypic organisms in a nano-reef with a water depth of less than 12 inches (30 cm). For many nano-reefs, these systems are the way to go. Smaller nano-reef aquaria may need to be illuminated by a single bulb due to space constraints; in these cases, look for a bulb that offers a color temperature somewhere between 6,500 and 10,000 Kelvin. This will provide adequate lighting for the growth and maintenance of coralline algae, macroalgae, and those corals and polyps with intermediate light intensity needs.

METAL HALIDES

Metal halide fixtures for nano-reefs are a recent introduction to the aquarium market. These units commonly utilize dual-ended 150-watt metal halide lamps to provide very intense light, albeit at the expense of increased energy consumption and heat production. A cooling fan incorporated into the fixture helps keep minimize the transfer of heat from the bulb to the water, but it still may not be enough to

prevent the water temperature from elevating above 82°F (28°C) during the day, which can be harmful if allowed to increase any higher than that. A small desktop fan set to blow air across the aquarium surface will help alleviate this problem. Halide bulbs paired with one or two actinic power compact bulbs results in a shimmering reef scene that would make even the most die-hard big-tank hobbyists envious!

Now that you've selected the lighting that best suits your livestock and the size of your nano-reef, you will need to make a decision regarding the **photoperiod** (the length of time that the lights are burning each day). There is little seasonal variation in the amount of time that tropical reefs receive illumination; the closer you get to the equator, the smaller the variation becomes. Approximately 12 hours of direct sunlight drench tropical reefs each day, so

Metal halide lighting is favored by many experienced hobbyists because of the intense light produced and the ripples of light that appear beneath the surface of the water. New hobbyists should be aware that the intense light produced by these bulbs is accompanied by intense heat, so the temperature of the aquarium water must be monitored and not allowed to exceed 82°F (28°C) for extended periods of time.

The Nano-Reef System

53

PART ONE

replicating this cycle on a reef aquarium is a sensible approach, and the easiest means of doing so is with a reliable timer. It is recommended that you determine the latest time that you want to be able to see the aquarium illuminated, and then work back 12 hours from there to set the time for the lights to turn on. For example, hobbyists who don't return home from the office each evening until 6 p.m. would get little enjoyment from their nano-reef if the lights were set to turn off just as they walked in the door each night. Therefore, they may decide to set the lights to turn on at 10 a.m. and off at 10 p.m., giving them time to observe the aquarium at their leisure.

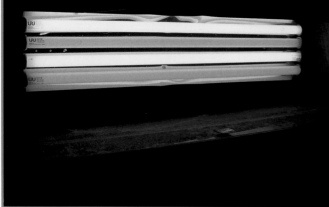

Canopies are an excellent way to hide the bulbs being used on the aquarium.

LEDs

The hobbyist looking to take his or her nano-reef to the limit will be interested in a light to simulate the lunar cycle, typically accomplished with one or more powerful LEDs of the proper Kelvin temperature. Several such light systems are available from high-end aquarium shops and online retailers, both incorporated into lighting canopies and as stand-alone units. A second (or third, depending on your setup) timer is used to control this "moon light," and turn it on an hour or so after the actinic bulbs in the aquarium have turned off; the moon light would then turn off some time in the early morning hours. For those truly enterprising hobbyists, a few minutes spent programming an electronic timer with multiple memory settings can provide a reasonable representation of an actual lunar cycle. If the nano-reef will be placed in a bedroom and you find the light emitted by a bright LED bothersome, it is prudent to skip the lunar simulation completely.

CANOPIES

Lighting canopies that feature a separate plug to operate bulbs of different Kelvin temperatures are available for nano-reef aquaria. When using one of these units, the hobbyist can simulate the changing light intensities and Kelvin temperatures associated with sunrise and sunset by using a timer to control each circuit. In this case, actinic bulbs would be set to turn on an hour earlier than the metal halide fixture, and remain on for one hour additional to the halide. To maintain the 12-hour photoperiod, the halide would therefore burn for 10 hours each day. A cooling fan would also be plugged into the timer controlling the halide fixture, circulating the air above the water when it is most needed. This dual-timer approach also works if two separate canopies are used (such as when employing a combination of power compact and metal halide lamps).

Having established the need for a cover, the question becomes, "What material should it be made of?" Two options are glass or acrylic and a light-diffuser grid (often referred to as an egg crate).

> ### Covers are a Must!
> Covering the top of the nano-reef with some sort of barrier serves a few functions:
> - It provides a surface upon which to place lighting fixtures manufactured for nano-reef aquaria, most of which do not have mounting brackets.
> - It prevents livestock from jumping out of the aquarium.
> - It prevents curious and uninformed observers from putting their fingers (or paws, as the case would most likely be; nano-reefs sitting on a tabletop or desktop are *particularly* accessible to feline friends) into the aquarium.

A solid glass or acrylic cover will allow light to pass through unobstructed and makes an attractive cover. If the aquarium's manufacturer does not offer a cover, one can be easily made either by providing the dimensions to a glass shop or by purchasing a piece of acrylic and cutting it to the proper dimensions with a fine-tooth saw.

Plastic light-diffuser material can be purchased by the sheet at home improvement centers and hardware stores, and it is easily cut into the proper dimensions using nothing more than a pair of steel side-cutters. The vertical slats of the grid taper from top to bottom. In order to maximize light transmission through the grid, place it so that the "fat end" of the slats are facing toward the light source. This material is available in white and chrome-painted colors. The reflective properties of the chrome finish produce the best results. However, the paint has a tendency to wear off with time unless treated; for that reason, try coating it with clear spray-epoxy once it has been cut down. The white plastic material does not require spray coating and still allows plenty of light to pass, so if this is all that is available at your local stores, don't think twice about purchasing it. Also, don't be too concerned about the plastic preventing enough light from entering the aquarium, because relatively little of the intensity is lost using either material. Expect to pay about 30–40% more for the chrome-painted material, which is still inexpensive at around $20 per panel (enough to make enclosures for several nano-reefs.

Plastic light diffusers have many uses in reef tanks—from shelving for live rock and corals to providing a place for the hood to rest.

One main consideration when deciding between a solid enclosure and one that allows air to freely pass through is the effect they have on water temperature. A solid enclosure inhibits evaporation, leading to an elevated water temperature. For reasons that will be explored in greater detail later, the elevating temperature limits the amount of dissolved oxygen that can exist in the water. Additionally, a solid top impedes gas exchange with the overlying air. This creates two problems. First, it limits the amount of oxygen entering the water. Second, it causes an increase in the water's dissolved CO_2 concentration. A deficiency in oxygen causes stress to aquatic organisms, something you obviously want to avoid. The buildup of CO_2 is also detrimental, not only because of its direct impact on the livestock's respiratory systems, but because it depresses pH and depletes alkalinity. An enclosure that allows free passage of gas, including water vapor, will alleviate the aforementioned problems. Whichever option you choose, be sure to leave a gap at the rear of the enclosure to enable placement of filtration equipment and electrical cords.

Regardless of the route you decide to take, properly illuminating a nano-reef is a relatively simple task, thanks to the array of lighting canopies available. As with other decisions regarding the purchase of equipment for your nano-reef, choose the best system that you can afford. You won't regret it.

Maintaining Tropical Water Temperatures

Water temperature on a tropical reef remains within a range of approximately 72–78°F (23-26°C) throughout the year, with short-term fluctuations occurring during periods of particularly dry or wet weather. Maintaining the water temperature of a reef aquarium within this range is highly recommended, though the temperature might be allowed to rise as high as 82°F (28°C) or fall as low as 70°F (21°C) for short periods of time without ample cause for concern. Most experienced reef aquarium hobbyists will attest to the difficulty of keeping the water below the maximum recommended value without the use of a chiller, and nano-reef aquaria offer no exception to this dilemma. The combination of lighting and one or more submersible water pumps or powerheads often creates excessive heat that drives the water temperature into the mid-80s°F (28-32°C) if not discouraged with vigorous air and water circulation at the water's surface. An electronic thermometer that enables the user to monitor the water temperature as well as that of the room is a worthy investment.

Novice reef hobbyists may ask why overheated water is of such great concern. The short answer is that long-term exposure to elevated water temperatures causes hermatypic corals to expel their zooxanthellae (known as "coral bleaching"), which almost always leads to their rapid death. This may be partly due to the lower oxygen concentration in the water that results from elevating

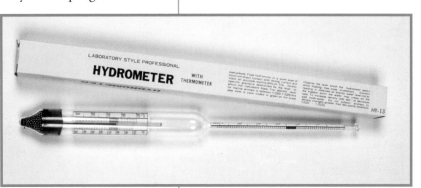

Floating hydrometers with a built-in thermometer are popular but may be a bit too large to use in a nano-reef.

Ricordia mushroom anemones are a rare and often expensive species that require very stable water conditions.

temperature[2], causing stress not only to corals but to the other livestock in the aquarium. Fish have a harder time obtaining sufficient oxygen and may be seen hovering at the surface of the water where the concentration of dissolved gas is greatest. In addition, this low-oxygen environment impacts the bacteria responsible for ammonia and nitrite oxidation, potentially causing mortality among the population that can lead to deteriorating water conditions. All points considered, it should be evident that avoiding prolonged elevated water temperature is an important aspect of maintaining any aquarium, regardless of size.

As alluded to above, circulation of water and air at the surface of the aquarium helps minimize the tendency for overheating. Exhaust from the protein skimmer and canister filter should be directed across the aquarium surface to provide turbulence and increase the rate of gas exchange with the water below. If only one of these filters is used on your nano-reef, a small submersible pump or powerhead with its exhaust directed across the surface of the water may be used for additional circulation. The use of a desktop fan such as the one discussed in the lighting section will encourage evaporation (which itself is full of energy in the form of heat) and carry heat away from the aquarium. If these measures still can't keep the water temperature within the recommended range, a chiller is needed.

CHILLERS

Experienced hobbyists are undoubtedly familiar with large chiller units used on aquaria over 50 gallons (189 l) in total volume, but as it turns out, there are smaller units that rely on thermoelectric technology to perform the same task. They utilize what is known as a Peltier element or circuit, which when powered causes one side of an element to get very cold and the other side to remove the heat. This heat is then conducted away from the hot side using a heat sink and fan. One such unit is capable of causing a temperature decrease of up to 8°F (5°C) in 10 gallons (37 l) of water, requires very little room, and is easily installed. Considering displacement of water from live rock and sand, one of these units should be capable of sufficiently cooling any nano-reef. All chillers must be used with a temperature regulator to cycle them on and off as needed.

Chillers are a must-have piece of equipment for nano-reefs that utilize metal halide lighting.

HEATERS

If your nano-reef happens to be situated in a room in which the air temperature is kept particularly cold, it might become necessary to utilize a heater to maintain the proper water temperature. The smallest submersible heater available to hobbyists is usually a 25-watt model, easily capable of providing all the heat needed. Even in the coldest of rooms, however, a nano-reef will probably remain within the safe temperature range without an additional heat source.

SEASONAL CHANGES

A final consideration on this topic is that changes in season and their associated effect on the temperature of your home (or wherever the nano-reef is situated) can dramatically impact water temperature extremes. You may find that the water temperature never rises above a comfortable 77°F (25°C) between late autumn and late spring, only to find it creeping toward the 84°F (29°C) mark (or higher) as summer wears on. In cases such as these, increase air movement across the top of the nano-reef as much as possible to increase the rate of evaporation, and note the impact this has on the water temperature. If the temperature is still staying too high for the safety

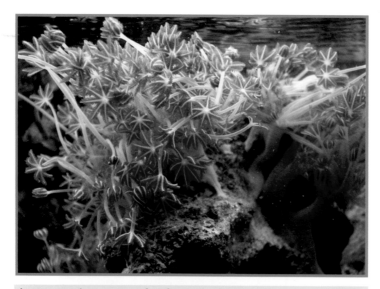

Long, waving types of soft corals like this Xenia coral need strong water movement in aquariums. The water movement will help remove wastes and detritus from in between the individual polyps and allow them access to fresh, clean water.

A Nano-Note on Wavemakers

I have no doubt that many aspiring hobbyists will entertain the idea of using a wave-making controller in their nano-reef to create the natural oscillation of the current found in the ocean. If you decide to go this route, use pumps with the lowest flow rate possible. In general, though, I think that this is taking things one step too far.

of the livestock, even if only for 30 minutes each day, you are wise to immediately begin researching a chiller such as the one discussed above. The extra money that you spend on this measure can easily save you several hundred dollars in replacing corals and other invertebrates that died as a direct result of these elevated water temperatures.

Water Movement

Throughout the preceding two sections, the impact that adequate water movement has in cooling the aquarium has been referred to. Turbulence at the water's surface caused when a flow of water interacts with an immobile object or with another water flow encourages the rapid exchange of gases between the water and the atmosphere. This turbulence also dislodges particulate organic material from live rock, live sand, and most importantly, the corals, clams, and other sessile (immobile) invertebrates in the nano-reef. Once the organic material enters the water column, it is easily removed by the mechanical filtration in place. Turbulence in a nano-reef should be enough to perform these tasks, yet not so violent that it causes particles of sand to become waterborne, corals to topple, or fish to struggle against the currents.

While the use of an air pump and air stone might seem reasonable to both create current and cool the water, it may not be suitable for nano-reefs housing corals and clams that are negatively impacted by the resulting microbubbles floating throughout the aquarium.

Accessories

In addition to all of the equipment discussed so far, some hobbyists might choose to investigate the use of a few *optional* instruments. For the hobbyists aspiring to have a truly high-tech nano-reef, these gadgets are at the top of their wish list. Although these high-tech systems are built to impress, the actual reef itself may not necessarily be any more picturesque than one set up with the bare essentials. However, this hobby is addictive, so purchasing a few hundred dollars of ancillary support equipment won't faze a lot of people!

Young leather corals will grow rapidly under the right conditions. pH, for example, is just one major chemical factor with which to be concerned.

The Nano-Reef System

61

PART ONE

One example of an electronic pH monitor. It's very important to check the pH of your nano-reef at least weekly.

pH MONITORS

The first item for consideration is an electronic pH monitor, which displays the pH in the system at all times. Calibration (which takes less than 10 minutes) every few months is recommended to ensure accuracy. Several manufacturers offer these units, both as enclosed pen-type models and those with a separate probe and display. A pH monitor can actually alert you to depleting alkalinity if you are observant—the greater the pH swing on a daily basis, the lower the alkalinity tends to be. Perform a formal test of the alkalinity in the nano-reef using an accurate test kit to determine the value and how much of the proper supplement is required to re-establish the level required for your particular system to maintain stable pH.

A CALCIUM REACTOR FOR A NANO-REEF?

How about a calcium reactor? Yes, for those truly high-tech hobbyists, there are small calcium reactors that could be used on a large nano-reef. Unless you're planning to build one yourself, however, the investment of several hundred dollars on one of these complete systems might actually be farther than even the most gadget-oriented hobbyists will venture.

DOSING SYSTEMS

A dosing system can continuously replace water lost to evaporation with no more than a few minutes of effort spent during initial setup. In addition to maintaining the salinity of the nano-reef, appropriate volumes of one or more supplements may be added to the reservoir to dose continuously. For example, small volumes of most

The rate of evaporation in nano-reefs can be astounding, requiring daily addition of fresh water to maintain stable salinity.

calcium, strontium, magnesium, trace element, and certain iodine supplements can be mixed together in the same container without any reactions to decrease their effectiveness. Gravity-fed dosing vessels are very simple in principle and operation: Adjust the drip rate of the water entering the nano-reef to maintain a stable water level. Though this takes some time to fine-tune, it enables you to take three-day (or longer) trips away from your aquarium without fear that you'll come back to find the aquarium half empty.

ORP Monitors

An ORP monitor is very useful in indicating the relative health of the system and alerting you to potential trouble before the livestock begin to show signs of stress. In a system as small as a nano-reef, this "early-warning" system can help avoid far-reaching problems with excessive organic material buildup and/or illness of livestock. Of all the accessories discussed in this section, an ORP monitor would be at the top of my wish list, followed by the pH monitor and then the drip-doser.

The Nano-Reef System

63

PART ONE

Chapter Three

Suggested Routine Maintenance

I n this day and age, spreadsheets seem to be needed in order to manage just about every aspect of life. Rather than write every observation you make in a notebook, why not create a spreadsheet that enables you to track the water parameters, the dates that livestock, light bulbs, and filtration media were purchased, notable changes in the livestock or general appearance of the nano-reef from day to day, and so on? Like so many hobbyists, you may spend the vast majority of each weekday in front of a computer. However, it is such a useful tool that a few additional minutes at the keyboard to help you remember important information is worth the sacrifice.

Maintenance Schedules

Maintenance can be divided into bi-weekly, weekly, and daily tasks. The extent to which you follow these suggestions is up to your discretion. However, it is recommended that you follow them as closely as possible for at least six months following setup of your nano-reef, if for no other reason than to familiarize yourself with the interactions of the livestock and the manner in which the filtration operates. Listed below are the maintenance checklists.

BI-WEEKLY MAINTENANCE

- Stir the live sand (if applicable) gently to liberate any particulate organic material, and remove it, either with a fine mesh net, by directing it toward the intake of the mechanical filter, or by removing it directly during the water change that follows.

- Perform a 25–50% water change using a quality synthetic sea salt and purified water. Remember to ensure that the temperature, salinity, and pH of the new water match the levels you maintain in the nano-reef *before* you begin any step of the water change.
- Clean caked salt off of surfaces above the water line with a damp cloth. Try not to let the salt fall into the water and land on sensitive invertebrates, such as corals and their allies, sponges, or the mantle tissue of clams and scallops.
- Rinse mechanical filtration media in the bucket of water you pulled from the reef during the water change, and then place the media back in the proper location.
- Inspect the protein skimmer and any additional filtration devices to determine whether or not they need to be temporarily disconnected and cleaned with a cloth and warm water.

WEEKLY MAINTENANCE

- Perform tests for calcium, alkalinity, and nitrate. If you are a stickler for knowing every possible important water parameter, perform additional tests for magnesium, strontium, and iodine.
- Check pH. Because pH values change during the course of the day, be sure to check the pH at the same time of day each week (i.e., 11 a.m.) to ensure standardized readings.
- Determine the volume of appropriate supplements needed to correct deficiencies. It is strongly recommended that you *not* dose the entire amount needed in one shot, but rather divide it by 7 and add this amount every day to maintain stability. It can be as easy as adding a few drops each day of a few different supplements, and doing this promotes awareness of how these supplements affect your nano-reef better than adding several supplements once each week. Remember that you can also add the appropriate amounts of supplements to a dosing device if you prefer.
- Empty the protein skimmer waste collection cup.

Checking the aquarium's salinity/ specific gravity can be done every other day.

DAILY MAINTENANCE

- Clean front and sides of aquarium with a magnet or scraper.
- Observe the livestock to ensure that they are healthy, vibrant, eating, and not molesting/being molested by other livestock. Perform a count of fishes and motile invertebrates to make certain that all are present.

- Feed livestock sparingly.
- Inspect live rock and live sand for signs of cyanobacteria and/or microalgae. If you spot either, remove as much as possible, perform a test for phosphate, and if present, begin taking steps to quickly decrease the phosphate concentration as well as that of latent organic material in the nano-reef. Assess your routine for possible sources of excess phosphate and correct the problem.
- Check salinity. (This can be performed every other day if you prefer.)
- Add supplements and water to replace that which has been lost to evaporation (if not using a dosing device).
- Check dosing device reservoir to ensure that it is filled with sufficient purified water to maintain salinity in the aquarium for at least two days.
- Check water temperature. Because the temperature of the aquarium is lowest before lights come on and highest after they have been burning for several hours, check the temperature at these times to make sure that it remains within the safe range.
- Check light bulbs, filters, pumps and/or powerheads to ensure that they are operating properly.

The daily list might seem extensive, but consider the fact that it only takes a few moments to glance over the entire system and make sure that all is in order. Checking the salinity and feeding the livestock can be accomplished in less than five minutes. The entire weekly list can typically be performed in under an hour, and the additional tasks of the bi-weekly list may add another 30 minutes to the process. (Remember, this is maintenance on an aquarium that might be as small as 1 gallon (3.78 l). The short period of time invested in maintenance is a very small price to pay for something that gives you, your family, and your friends so many hours of enjoyment.

A hand-held algae scraper will make cleaning your aquarium's glass a quick and easy task that can be accomplished in minutes.

There are a few additional tasks that should be mentioned. If using a pH monitor, be sure to calibrate it once every six months or so using the solution provided by the manufacturer of the unit. Tubing used in dosing units should also be inspected at that time and cleaned if mineral buildup is present.

Photographing the aquarium at least once a month or more to create a photo journal of the changes in the appearance of the system is a great idea, even if only just for your own records and to show your friends.

Many hobbyists spend a great deal of time researching and planning a new aquarium, but then they set it up and become bored of it within a few months. A major cause of this phenomenon is that these hobbyists cease to perform daily, weekly, and even bi-weekly maintenance on their aquaria, leading to a general loss of interest. Not long thereafter, livestock begin to suffer and perish. Consider the fact that you alone are responsible for keeping these creatures from the wild alive, and that without your care they will live very short, unpleasant lives in captivity. Make every effort to perform the maintenance required for the long-term success of your aquarium, and you will be rewarded with a display to be proud of. After all, no aquarium takes care of itself.

Congratulations! You've made it through the dizzying and sometimes complicated array of information that is the life support of every marine aquarium. From here, the livestock itself will be explored, and those groups of fishes and invertebrates that are most likely to make amiable nano-reef residents will be highlighted.

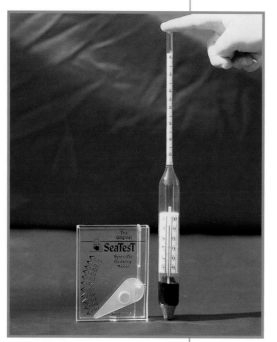

Examples of a swing-arm hydrometer (left) and combination thermometer and hydrometer. The former is dipped into the aquarium and reads salinity directly, whereas the latter is placed in a tall tube into which a sample of aquarium water is poured for the measurement to take place.

The fishes that you add to your nano-reef system should be hardy and easy to care for. Species like this mandarinfish (Synchiropus splendidus) *are not always the best choice but sometimes certain specimens do very well.*

Chapter Four

Sensible Stocking

There are few environments on Earth that boast such a diverse and colorful array of organisms as tropical coral reefs. True, the African Great Lakes boast tons of colorful cichlids, and rainforest streams teem with vibrant characins and abundant plant growth, but in the aquatic realm, coral reefs stand alone as the pinnacle of creation.

Avoiding the "Three O's": Overstocking, Overcrowding, and Overfeeding

Some might consider it semantics, but herein overcrowding and overstocking are treated as two different things, though both can result in dead livestock and should therefore be avoided at all costs. **Overstocking** is a state in which an overabundance of life (usually restricted to animal life) in the aquarium produces waste materials at a faster rate than the filtration system can detoxify or remove them. **Overcrowding** is a different state, one in which the proximity of the organisms causes aggressive, and potentially lethal, interactions. **Overfeeding** should be familiar to those readers who used to watch their favorite "neighbor" on public television feed his fish every morning by wantonly dumping what seemed to be half a can of flakes into the aquarium; note to self: don't try this at home. There's a reason that those fish seemed to look different every other episode!

When small colonies of soft corals grow, they can quickly become larger than the nano-reef can handle. Care must be taken that your corals are fragged out or clipped back as needed.

OVERSTOCKING

Consider a 5-gallon (18.95-l) nano-reef housing a group of six juvenile percula anemonefish (*Amphiprion percula*). While young, the fish consume a modest amount of food each day. The hobbyist pays special attention to feed the fishes only as much as they can consume in two minutes, no food appears to go uneaten, and the live rock and protein skimmer in place maintain ammonia, nitrite, and phosphate at immeasurable concentrations. However, as weeks pass and the hobbyist follows the same routine, the concentrations of these pollutants rise, causing the fish to become ill. The hobbyist does a large water change, then purchases a small canister filter and loads it with a blend of activated carbon and ion-exchange resin to bolster filtration. For a few weeks, the water parameters seem to be stable, with no measurable pollutants, but then ammonia and nitrite concentrations start creeping upward and the fish once again look ill. This is a classic case of overstocking, and the only solution to this problem in a nano-reef is to remove some of the fish, lowering the amount of food that must be added to the tank each day.

OVERCROWDING

Consider the same nano-reef with three soft corals and a large colony of star polyps. Placed in different locations in the aquarium, the corals and polyps are not in direct physical contact with one another and are at peace. The hobbyist maintains the water parameters within the recommended ranges and faithfully changes a gallon (3.79 l) of water each week, and the environment encourages the growth of his precious and beautiful livestock. Several months later, the nano-reef appears very different and mature, as corals, polyps, and coralline algae have grown to occupy much more space. The problem now is that two of the corals are beginning to touch each other when the current catches them just the right way, and the tissue of one coral is beginning to look white, crumbling or disintegrating away when touched. The same thing is happening where the star polyps are touching the third coral. This is a case of overcrowding, which can be remedied by pruning the corals and polyps as needed to prevent them from touching. (This practice also creates "daughter colonies" that may be transplanted to other aquaria.) The problem is ultimately related to the fact that toxins injected by nematocysts vary in strength with different species of octocorals; some are relatively innocuous, while

While schools of marine fishes are interesting to observe, they often need a lot of room. Nano-reefs are not good aquariums for schooling fishes on average, so such animals are best left for those who can provide tanks large enough to house them properly.

others are particularly volatile, and as you might expect, there are corals that fall in the range between these two extremes. Prevent the corals and polyps from coming into direct contact, and you can avoid this particular problem.

OVERFEEDING

The basic rule that has been around the aquarium hobby for years is to only feed what your fish can eat in a few minutes. When feeding flakes, pellets, or some other prepared food, following such a rule isn't that difficult—even with little experience. Today, however, hobbyists run into two problems with this rule: first, there are more varieties of foods to choose from now than ever before, and not all of them are easily monitored once they hit the water; second, reef hobbyists are encouraged to feed corals and other invertebrates with foods that cannot possibly be

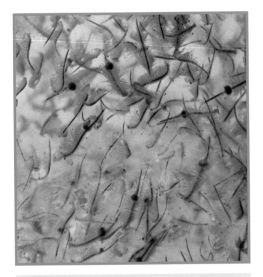

Brine shrimp are commonly used as a live food, especially for dragonets and dartfishes.

Hermit crabs are a must-have for the nano-reef setup.

Using Hermit Crabs to Your Advantage

One of the great roles that hermit crabs play in the reef aquarium is as active scavengers of whatever edible items they can get their claws on; it's not uncommon to observe hermits of various species in reef aquaria sprinting across gravel and hurdling each other to capture particles of food drifting in the current. On this point alone, the presence of hermit crabs in a marine aquarium, regardless of volume, is warranted.

completely accounted for once they have entered the system. Feeding the invertebrates is in addition to feeding the fish, making it very easy to pollute the system even though your efforts are with good intentions.

Even with advances in filtration and the understanding of chemical and biological reactions taking place within a marine aquarium, it is just as important to limit the amount of latent organic material entering the system now as it was in decades past. No matter what sort(s) of food are employed, feeding the fish once or twice a day (at most) and limiting the feeding to one type of food per session is still recommended. Try to follow the "few minutes" rule.

Foods for invertebrates are largely formulated with plankton and protein solids. If the aquarium houses any ahermatypic filter feeders, the occasional use of these foods is justified since without regular feeding, the animals will perish. By the same token, hermatypic invertebrates maintained in aquaria with light intensity insufficient to maintain the harvesting of food from their symbiotic zooxanthellae will require infrequent feeding. Note the choice of words: "occasional" and "infrequent". Overuse of these products will degrade water quality in any aquarium, regardless of the overall system volume. The nano-reef hobbyist has a major strike against them from the beginning: the volume of water in their aquarium is so minimal that any uneaten organic material will rapidly decay and lead to elevated concentrations of ammonia and phosphate. It's possible that the effects of overfeeding can be minimized by employing effective protein skimmers and/or using organic adsorption resins and phosphate-removal media, but why spend money to fix problems that can be completely and simply avoided by feeding frugally? All of that being stated, feeding invertebrates a few drops of food once every other day is all that a reef may require. Observe the appearance of the livestock after feeding to determine whether the amount was insufficient, "just right," or excessive, then alter the feeding next time (if needed) to correct problems.

Choosing Livestock Wisely

The inhabitants of the reefs have spent millions of years developing mechanisms to exclude species that they regard as competition for space and food from their general vicinity. This is not only limited to fish and motile invertebrates. Many species of corals and their allies aggressively defend their immediate surroundings against encroaching coral colonies by physical attack or chemical warfare. When the method of attack is with special tentacles densely armed with batteries of stinging cells, the end result is damaged tissue to the encroacher that, within the confines of an aquarium, may become infected with bacteria that ultimately wipe out the entire colony. Chemicals excreted by some types of corals, notably those of the genera *Cladiella* (which includes the colt coral) and *Lemnalia* (which includes the tree and cauliflower corals), can gradually kill many species of corals located down-current. Stony corals are among those that will fall victim to these coral chemical factories, making the

Two examples of "star polyps." The colony in the foreground is actually a stalk of Briareum *sp. originating in the Caribbean, while the background colony originated in the Western Pacific. Colonies such as these make colorful and interesting nano-reef residents.*

Livestock

75

PART TWO

cohabitation of these groups of corals in even the largest of aquaria a very risky proposition. These and other incompatible organisms encounter each other in nature all the time, and they may survive long enough to procreate, but the long-term survival outlook for the unfortunate individual coral colonies is bleak. This is not something that should be replicated within the hobbyist's aquaria. Consider how hard it might be to crowd compatible fishes and invertebrates together in a 120-gallon (454-l) aquarium to the extent that their forced close association creates conflict and leads to the death of livestock. This is probably pretty difficult to accomplish in a short period of time, right? Not so with an aquarium $1/10$ that size or even smaller. Your decisions regarding which corals, colonial and solitary polyps, clams and other bivalves, snails and other gastropods, crustaceans, and fishes to place into this tiny ecosystem must be made carefully and intelligently to avoid as much conflict as possible.

When choosing fishes and motile invertebrates, some keys to making intelligent decisions are as follows:
- Do not house organisms known to prey on one another in the same aquarium. This may seem elementary, but more than one ornamental shrimp has become a quick meal for a hawkfish, dottyback, or basslet small enough to be placed into a large nano-reef, though the hobbyist may have thought the fish incapable of such an act.
- Unless the aquarium is large enough or it is generally accepted that members of the same species (**conspecifics**) may be housed together, stick to one individual of a species per aquarium. Ignoring this rule often leads to a series of aggressive confrontations between the organisms in question, as they regard each other as a threat to their territory or resources for food and (if of the same sex) a mate. A very good example is the coral-banded or boxer shrimp (*Stenopus hispidus*), which (unless a mated pair) will usually kill each other in short order once placed in the same aquarium. This rule applies equally

Coral-banded shrimp, shown here, are best maintained individually in all but the largest marine aquaria, unless there is a confirmed mated pair; in all other cases, a pair of these shrimp placed into the same aquarium will fight incessantly until only one remains. Often the victor is so badly hurt that it, too, perishes.

to fish. Most reef fishes don't appreciate the presence of conspecifics in the same aquarium, unless they happen to be a mated pair or the amount of room available to them permits an "out of sight, out of mind" lifestyle. In nano-reef aquaria, this is never the case.

Various zoanthids make wonderful fillers for empty areas of a nano-reef aquarium. They are usually very peaceful, but they do need to be fed.

- Do not place fishes of the same body shape and/or coloration together in a small aquarium. As noted above, the perceived competition for available resources will lead to confrontation and a very unpleasant demise for the loser.
- Do not house species of fish noted for being particularly timid with those noted to be overly aggressive. An example of this case would be attempting to keep a firefish in the same aquarium with a dottyback; the firefish will inevitably wind up on the floor or simply in pieces.
- Research the dwelling habits of livestock (i.e. where they tend to hang out most of the time, such as in caves, near the top of the aquarium, out in the open, on the substrate, etc.), and do not house species together that share the same preferences *unless* sufficient space exists in the aquarium to keep both individuals happy. The firefish/dottyback example above could illustrate this point very well, also.
- Apply the rule above to feeding habits. No matter how different they appear, a pair of dwarf wrasse, for instance, in the same aquarium, is apt to spend much of the day browsing over the same pieces of rock in search of microinvertebrates upon which to feed; this greatly increases the probability of an aggressive confrontation between the two fish.

- Research the feeding habits and movements of motile invertebrates, and exclude those species that have been noted to occasionally feed on corals and their allies (such as various species of sea stars), as well as those that have a tendency to topple corals and rockwork (such as sea urchins).

When choosing sessile invertebrates for any reef aquarium, keep the following in mind:

- Housing octocorals and stony corals (**scleractinians**) together in the same system presents problems that can only be effectively dealt with by the dilution of toxins into a very large volume of water and through the use of aggressive chemical filtration. This assumes that water passes through the filtration *before* the toxins reach the stony coral, which is not always the case. In the confines of a nano-reef, it is best to limit your choice of corals to keeping octocorals *or* scleractinians, but not mixing them together. Both of these groups may, however, be mixed with **zoanthideans** (or zoanthids, as they are commonly called; these are the colorful colonial and solitary polyps that often look like miniature anemones) safely, as long as they are not in direct physical contact. Mushroom anemones and their allies (the **corallimorpharians**, or corallimorphs, collectively) are also known to produce toxins and are best housed with octocorals and zoanthids in nano-reef aquaria. Leave the scleractinians out of such a system. I have found, in fact, that when keeping stony corals in a nano-reef, it is best to keep them only with other scleractinians rather than mixing them with the other orders of the coral class[1].

- Attention must be paid to the rate at which corals and their allies are known to grow under ideal conditions, and that knowledge applied to the physical placement of colonies and polyps in the aquarium so

Sun polyps often do poorly in captivity. Therefore, it is probably best not to buy them for your nano-reef.

they don't come within reach of each other .
On the positive side of things, if these
organisms are growing at such a rate that it
becomes a regular task to move colonies to
prevent their contact, you are doing
something right. You can either start making
fragments and cuttings of the original colonies
to keep them from touching and stock
another aquarium or sell/trade them to/with
fellow hobbyists, or you can simply remove
some of the colonies to create more space for
others in the aquarium to grow. The extended
polyps of several octocorals and scleractinians
may reach well over 3 inches (7.5 cm) from
the base of the colony, so providing ample
room between specimens is necessary. Note
that many species of large-polyped stony
corals extend specialized sweeper tentacles at
night to kill encroaching coral species—they
must be situated several inches from their
nearest coral neighbors if conflict is to be
avoided. In the confines of a nano-reef
aquarium, there simply may not be sufficient
space to safely house these species.

- Learn about the feeding requirements of each
species you are interested in. While most species of corals and
polyps offered for sale in the aquarium hobby are hermatypic,
there are a few particularly beautiful ones that are not (these
groups lack symbiotic zooxanthellae, and are referred to as
ahermatypic) and that require regular feeding to remain
healthy. Corals of the genus *Tubastraea* (sun polyps) and
Dendronephthya (cauliflower corals) are commonly seen in
stores. However, their long-term survival rate in captivity is
quite poor, with colonies often surviving less than three months
because the hobbyist is not providing them with proper food

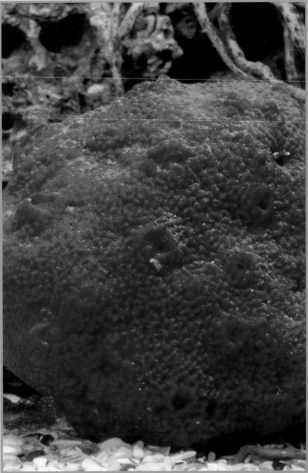

*Sponges, while often beautiful and
unique, require frequent feedings and
are best reserved for those hobbyists
who have the setups that such
animals require.*

The stalk of Xenia *shown is one of more than 50 that split off of another stalk as individual heads less than six months prior to taking this photo. To say that* Xenia *sp. can be prolific in captivity is something of an understatement.*

items in adequate amounts to maintain their health. This in itself may simply be because the concentration of organic material in the aquarium gets out of hand as a result of the food influx in the aquarium. I recommend that these and other ahermatypic corals be placed only in systems with high-capacity protein skimmers and a lot of water, both of which help maintain low concentrations of organic material in heavily fed aquaria. These corals truly are best left to hobbyists with actual experience in their successful husbandry. The same applies to many species of anemones commonly encountered in stores. Though they are hermatypic, most experts will agree that anemones fare much better when given regular feedings. Sponges are yet another great example of organisms that require frequent feeding in order to survive. Why risk the life of an organism that your aquarium just isn't equipped to maintain over the long term?

- Related to the previous point, try to house organisms that have the same or similar feeding requirements together, rather than maintaining a collection of animals that feed on totally different items. In an aquarium with this feeding diversity, a hobbyist must provide adequate densities of several different types of food to ensure long-term survival of the livestock. Although the total amount of food needed in this system may be the same regardless of average prey size, the need for a complex feeding regimen encourages overfeeding, which as mentioned earlier, should be expressly avoided in a nano-reef.

- Take note of species that are known to wander around the aquarium until they've found a suitable location. This is a reference to true anemones (actinarians), as many readers might suspect, though I have had great experience with colonies of *Xenia* moving slowly from place to place, presumably for the same reasons their anemone cousins do: in order to find better lighting and/or water movement. Of the true anemones, Bulb or bubble-tip anemones (*Entacmaea quadricolor*) and Ritteri or magnificent anemones (*Heteractis magnifica*) are a couple of noteworthy travelers, often traversing an entire rock wall in the course of an evening. (They seem to limit this wandering to nighttime). By comparison, it would take *Xenia* several days or even weeks to move the same distance, but this slow rate of movement makes it all the more difficult to actually detect (until one day you look at the colony and realize it is several inches [centimeters] from where it was the week before).

The danger is two-fold. First, if these organisms get too near the intake of a powerhead or submerged pump, they can easily become sucked in and macerated (they are, after all, essentially bags of water and have no skeletal structure to speak of), killing them and distributing their contents throughout the aquarium. A large-scale water change will then need to be performed and augmented chemical filtration put in place to minimize the impact on water quality and the rest of the aquarium livestock. The second problem is that a wandering anemone or *Xenia* colony can sting and be stung by other anemones, polyps, and corals, causing damage to tissue that can lead to the death of an individual or colony. Anemones have a mind of their own and move surprisingly quickly (a few inches [centimeters] per hour) for a hobbyist with no experience in their captive care, so it is not uncommon to go to bed with an animal at the foot of the reef and wake to find it sitting on a spray bar near the surface, over 12 inches (30 cm) in vertical distance from where it had been several hours before. In fact, they rarely stay where the hobbyist places them initially. This being the case, if you insist on keeping an anemone in your nano-reef, exclude stony corals from the aquarium. They seem to be easily damaged by most anemones (particularly anemones of the genera *Stichodactyla* and *Condylactis*); by contrast, many species of solitary and colonial polyps may tolerate physical contact with these animals. If your desire is to keep a pair of anemonefish in the nano-reef and want an anemone host for

These strikingly beautiful blue mushrooms are a rare treat and can be quite expensive—even for mushrooms. However, they do as well in nano-reefs as do most other corallimorpharians.

Six Steps to Sensibly Stocking a Nano-Reef

A nano-reef is such a confined space that it can be simple to overstock it with fishes and invertebrates. If, however, the hobbyist follows a series of steps when setting up a new nano-reef, a suitable stocking density of ornamental marine organisms can easily be achieved. Following are some general guidelines for long-term success when initially stocking a nano-reef:

- Use approximately 1 lb (0.4536 kg) of highly porous, low-density cured live rock per gallon (3.79 l) of total water capacity in the aquarium, depending on how much open space you want in the nano-reef. This is the basis that will determine where you place sessile invertebrates.
- Place no more than one octocoral of a given genus in the aquarium per 2.5–3.0 gallons (9.475–11.37 l) of total water capacity. For example, because they are generally compatible with each other, toadstool corals of the genus S*arcophyton* can be maintained together with little concern of "chemical warfare," though they should still be kept physically separated to allow full polyp extension.
- Regardless of their initial size, place no more than one individual octocoral in the aquarium per 2.5–3.0 gallons (9.475-11.37 l) of total water capacity. Smaller corals are significantly cheaper than larger specimens.
- If you plan to stock the reef with fragments of small-polyped stony corals, allow a distance of *at least* 2 inches (5 cm) from each neighboring frag. This will enable the colonies to grow for at least one year without undue concern that they will come into contact with one another.

- Place no more than one ornamental shrimp or "nano-reef-compatible" fish per 3 gallons (11.37 l) of total water capacity into the aquarium. Before placing conspecifics into the same aquarium, research their tolerance of each other in captivity. Otherwise, you will undoubtedly witness "aquatic homicide."
- Utilize no more than one scarlet reef hermit crab (*Paguristes* sp.), three blue-leg or red-leg hermit crabs (*Clibanarius* sp.), and one tropical abalone or limpet per 5 gallons (18.95 l) of total water capacity as an algae and detritus cleaning group.

There will be a discussion later of the groups of animals considered suitable for housing in a nano-reef in greater detail shortly. For now, take these suggestions into consideration and try to plan your new nano-reef accordingly. A properly stocked and well-planned nano-reef can be a beautiful and frustration-free aquarium!

them, try investigating a recognized anemone alternative, such as the smaller varieties of *Rhodactis* sp. mushroom anemones, that tend to stay in one place.

- Some of the octocorals, zoanthids, and corallimorphs reproduce at a surprising rate under optimal conditions. Of these, *Xenia* appears to be the most prolific. In my own aquaria, I have witnessed well over 50 large, individual new colonies of *Xenia* produced from just two stalks within the span of 6 months, without actively encouraging them to proliferate. These colonies tend to settle in places that I would prefer they not be, such as in the middle of a colony of zoanthids or on the shell of a live Tridacnid clam. It is therefore necessary to monitor their reproduction in a nano-reef and remove colonies as necessary. By contrast, the rest of the members of these orders reproduce relatively slowly, but still enough to warrant monitoring in a nano-reef. Ensure that new colonies or individuals will not come into contact with more delicate or aggressive relatives. Aquaria housing only corallimorphs, zoanthids, or members of the same species don't have this problem, as they are generally compatible with one another.
- You cannot, of course, plan for every contingency; there will be times that animals behave uncharacteristically, with an unpleasant end result. The frequency of these occurrences is minimized by familiarizing yourself with the "normal" behavior

These young leather corals are very healthy, which is evident by their color and how "open" they are.

and care requirements for all the organisms you're interested in keeping. This applies to all aquaria, not just nano-reefs.

Selecting Healthy Livestock

Selecting healthy livestock from your local aquarium store involves making a mental checklist and being certain that the organism in question meets all requirements before putting your cash or credit card on the counter and committing to the purchase.

The physical appearance of the organism is the first thing you will notice. In fish, eyes should be clear (i.e., free of cloudiness or white patches); both eyes should be present; fins should be largely intact and not overly torn; there should be no signs of illness, redness, white patches, ectoparasites (such as ich or velvet), or emaciation (i.e., pinched-in areas behind the head or in the stomach area); coloration should be normal (stressed coloration in many fishes differs markedly from the normal coloration); the fish should be alert and able to maintain its buoyancy and orientation normally (not floating to the surface or uncharacteristically sinking to the bottom and having trouble staying upright); and it should eat when appropriate food is added to the aquarium (provided it hasn't just been fed). Decorative crabs and shrimp should have both eyes and all limbs, though limbs and antennae will grow back when the animal molts. Corals and their allies should show absolutely no signs of tissue damage or degeneration whatsoever. They should also be inspected in the dealer's aquarium for flatworms, visible amphipods (appearing as tiny red "bug-like" creatures), and other unwanted hitchhikers. If *any* of these items don't check out, you are at much greater risk of the organism not surviving very long once it has been placed in your aquarium than you would be by selecting a truly healthy specimen.

Quarantining New Livestock

Many aquarium shops and dealers will quarantine new livestock for a period of days or even weeks before they are offered for sale. This ensures that the animals are indeed healthy before hobbyists take them home and minimizes the number of needless fatalities that are the result of moving an animal from system to system too soon after it has gone through the trauma of being shipped halfway across the globe. Purchasing livestock that has been quarantined for at least a week is a sensible measure of precaution to take.

A mixture of soft and stony corals, zoanthids, and even the occasional clam is the "look" that most nano-reefers are going for.

Chapter Five

Fishes for Nano-Reef Aquariums

Due to its diminutive volume, a nano-reef imposes several physical and behavioral requirements on fish that must be met for successful long-term care. First, the maximum adult size of the species should *generally* be no more than 3 inches (7.5 cm) in total length[1]; nano-reef aquaria 5 gallons (18.95 l) or less in total volume can comfortably support fish no more than 1 inch (2.5 cm) in total length. In these very small systems, I usually skip fish and stock them with one or two colorful shrimp instead.

Second, the species should ideally be able to obtain part of its food from browsing over live rock and live sand (if present) in an established aquarium to decrease the need for daily feedings, hence lowering the associated impact on water quality. Third, the species must be generally considered as safe to house with the ornamental invertebrates present in the aquarium. This does not mean that all fishes not considered as "reef safe" are excluded from reef aquaria, just that they shouldn't be housed with *certain types* of invertebrates. For example, a species considered a threat to the mantles of Tridacnid clams may ignore the tissue of small-polyped stony corals. Within families, different species will show different preferences for feeding on invertebrates, and this can even vary within species, as individuals behave somewhat differently.

Fourth, the species should be relatively disease resistant and able to withstand moderate fluctuations in water quality.

In addition, it helps if the fish performs some specific purpose in the nano-reef (e.g., algae-eating or sand-sifting). Whereas a fish-only aquarium is little more than a tank displaying pretty fish, a natural coral reef is an operating ecosystem in which all inhabitants play some role or perform a job. There are three main categories or job roles that fish play in reef aquaria:

- **Substrate-sifter**—Keeps live sand free of impacted organic material by continuously taking mouthfuls and sifting it. Note that this fish cannot be a homebody; rather, it must be a "free-range" fish that has no qualms about searching every square inch of substrate in the tank for a meal. In other words, shrimp gobies and jawfishes need not apply. The twinspot or signal goby (*Signigobius biocellatus*) and Hector's goby (*Amblyeleotris hectori*) are suitable choices for nano-reef aquaria.

- **Algae-grazer**—This position must be filled by a fish that actively browses the live rock, live sand, sessile invertebrates, and aquarium surfaces for edible varieties of algae. The fish need not necessarily eat every sort of algae present in the aquarium, but flexibility of diet is greatly valued. Once again, Hector's goby (*Amblyeleotris hectori*) will perform this task admirably. Damselfishes of the genus *Chrysiptera* are perfect for this task, though they tend to be aggressive, so exercise due caution with tankmate selection.

- **Microinvertebrate-grazer**—Spends every waking hour thoroughly browsing over and through each nook and cranny in the live rock for minute invertebrates such

The royal gramma (Gramma loreto), *a microinvertebrate grazer, needs to be fed small invertebrates in order to thrive in the nano-reef aquarium.*

as small bristleworms, copepods, amphipods, isopods, pyramidellid snails, flatworms, predatory nudibranchs, and the like. As you might expect, strong preference is shown for species that do not normally view larger gastropods and crustaceans as potential meals (though unwelcome mantis shrimp are a welcome exception). Special consideration is given to species that help control ectoparasites on tankmates. This group has the most nano-reef-compatible species.

Do Your Research

I suggest that you spend some time reading the general descriptions provided and then reference one or more books that specifically address the characteristics of nano-ree-compatible fishes before making any final decisions. The most success invariably comes from choosing tankmates of an even-temperament that do not resemble each other in body shape, coloration, feeding habits (whenever possible), and area of the aquarium that they spend the most time in (i.e., bottom-dwellers vs. fish that stay in the upper third of the aquarium).

The sixline wrasse (*Pseudocheilinus hexataenia*) is one of my all-time favorite species and the perfect microinvertebrate-grazer in my experience discussed in some detail in the following section. Other notable species are Rainford's goby (*Amblygobius rainfordi*) and the Swissguard basslet (*Liopropoma rubre*). Many of the smaller members of the dottybacks (*Pseudochrmidae*), reef basslets (*Liopropomini*), basslets (*Grammatidae*), and fairy wrasse (various genera) can fulfill this function, so take your time and choose species that appeal to you and are safe with the ornamental invertebrates you wish to keep.

Of course, every fish in the nano-reef needn't necessarily have a specific function; it might just be pretty or exhibit behavior that you find interesting. There are many nano-reef-compatible species that fit this description.

Not only is it important to choose fish tankmates wisely, but they must also be selected in terms of their compatibility with invertebrates that are to be housed in the aquarium. This doesn't just apply to whether the fishes are likely to harass the invertebrates, but it also applies to whether the invertebrates are likely to eat the fish! For example, elephant ear mushroom anemones (*Rhodactis* sp.) make frequent meals of fish that have a habit of perching and resting for lengthy periods of time; therefore, many gobies, blennies, and hawkfishes are prime targets. The message here is to simply avoid placing these corallimorphs and perching fishes in the same aquarium.

Livestock

89

PART TWO

Pygmy angelfishes, such as the coral beauty (*Centropyge bispinosus*) shown, may be housed in the largest aquaria falling under the nano-reef heading, but they are truly better placed into larger aquaria with inherently more stable water chemistry for long-term care.

Suggested Fishes for the Nano-Reef Aquarium

The following are general descriptions of many species of fishes and their families that are good candidates for nano-reef life. Unless expressly noted, all species discussed should be kept as solitary members of their family in a nano-reef to avoid fighting; that is to say that more than one fish of the same family should *not* be kept in the same nano-reef.

DWARF ANGELFISHES / FAMILY POMACANTHIDAE

The **angelfishes** are a diverse family in terms of maximum size, coloration, and behavior. The family can be divided between two "main groups"—those that attain lengths greater than 6 inches (15.5 cm) when fully grown and those that remain smaller. The hobbyist's main attraction to this family is the seemingly endless variety of color and pattern combinations among the members. The "personality" of this group is also alluring. These fishes may also become somewhat tame, even taking food out of their keeper's hands.

A Nano-Note on Pygmy Angels

I have found several species of pygmy angelfishes to be safe with invertebrates in most nano-reefs, though I believe that they should only be placed in larger nano-reef aquaria.

The dwarf angelfishes of the genus *Centropyge* compose many beautiful species. Unlike juveniles of the larger angelfish species, most dwarf angels do not undergo a color change associated with age. This is not a hard rule, though, and there are some color variants of species that have been observed. Additionally, a few species are known to hybridize, creating unique individuals that are quite rare in the aquarium hobby and beautiful to behold. For the most part, however, changes in shade of color are typically related to mood, stress, or sleep. Nearly all dwarf angels range in maximum length from a diminutive 2 inches (5 cm) to a little more than 7 inches (17.5 cm); it is the smaller species we're interested in for nano-reef residency. The pygmy cherub angelfish (*Centropyge argi*), African flameback angelfish (*C. acanthops*), Brazilian flameback or fireball angelfish (*C. aurantonotus*), and Fisher's angelfish (*C. fisheri*) remain smaller than 3 inches

(7.5 cm) in total length (TL) and are generally considered "reef safe."

The remaining species of pygmy angelfishes either grow too large for placement in nano-reefs or display less than ideal feeding behavior when it comes to invertebrates. Even angelfishes regarded as being reef safe are known to browse indiscriminately on sponges and the soft tissue of corals and clams from time to time, so be sure to monitor these nano-reef residents just as a cautionary measure.

For the most part, angelfishes are a tough group. Members of this family might be best labeled as "assertive" rather than aggressive. Best added to an aquarium last, they will quickly establish themselves either as the ruler of the fishes or a formidable opponent, and they rarely back down to non-angelfish species of an aggressive disposition. They will, however, generally leave tankmates not considered a threat or competitor alone once dominance has been established, thus usually making these angelfishes peaceful inhabitants with most mild-mannered species.

WRASSES / FAMILY LABRIDAE

Wrasses compose a very large family of fishes, with over 400 species identified. They are in the same superorder as cichlids and damselfishes, interestingly, due to dental morphology. The group can be divided into those species that are generally reef safe and those that are not.

The members of the family making up the reef-safe group generally remain smaller than 5 inches (12.5 cm) as adults. Some of the more commonly available species are

The cleaner wrasse (Labroides dimidiatus) *is a commonly available species that is difficult to rear in any captive system.*

of the genera *Cirrhilabrus*, *Halichoeres*, *Labroides*, *Macropharyngodon*, *Paracheilinus*, and *Pseudocheilinus*. Collectively, these species might also be referred to as "dwarf wrasses." It should be noted that some species can be very difficult to maintain in captivity due either to the inability of the hobbyist to meet their general feeding requirements or to stress incurred during shipping that causes the fish to perish. Notable examples are the cleaner and leopard wrasses of the genera *Labroides* and *Macropharyngodon*, respectively, which have very poor survival records in captivity.

Bristleworms, such as the one shown above, are fed upon by many species of wrasse. It is important to note that bristleworms play an important role in all marine aquaria by scavenging organic matter in very tight places, thereby helping convert that material into biomass and decreasing the impact it has on water quality.

With few exceptions, the remaining members of the group are fairly easy to maintain under proper conditions. They are all quite hardy, have simple feeding requirements, and are generally disease resistant. In addition, the variety of colors and patterns is seemingly endless, and many species are relatively inexpensive.

In general, these wrasses feed mainly on tiny invertebrates found in rocks and among the polyps and branches of corals. Their days are spent searching through every crack and crevice in the aquarium for prey, and their nights are generally spent buried beneath the sand where they are safe from most nocturnal predators. Harmless to practically all desirable invertebrates[2] and other fish, many of the dwarf wrasses make ideal residents for nano-reef aquaria. They are very good at removing pests such as bristleworms, flatworms, and planarians from the aquarium in their never-ending quest for a meal. They can be fed brine shrimp, zooplankton, and minced fish and shrimp as a supplement to the organisms they find by browsing. Bristleworms, arriving as stowaways on corals, can be fed directly to wrasses. You can drop them into the water and then watch as the wrasse grabs one end of the worm and slurps it in like a piece of spaghetti.

Some of the durable species commonly available at retailers are the twinspot hogfish (*Bodianus bimaculatus*), whipfin fairy wrasse (*Cirrhilabrus filamentosus*), Lubbock's fairy wrasse (*C. lubbocki*), yellow-flanked fairy wrasse (*C. lyukyuensis*), fine-spotted fairy wrasse (*C. punctatus*), longfin fairy wrasse (*C. rubriventralis*), redfin fairy wrasse (*C. rubripinnis*), red velvet fairy wrasse (*C. rubrisquamis*), Scott's fairy wrasse (*C. scottorum*), solar fairy wrasse (*C. solorensis*), golden wrasse

(*Halichoeres chrysus*), radiant wrasse (*H. iridis*), neon wrasse (*H. melanurus*), all flasher wrasses of the genus *Paracheilinus* (of which at least nine species are occasionally seen in stores), sixline wrasse (*Pseudocheilinus hexataenia*), and fourline wrasse (*P. tetrataenia*). In addition, there are many more species being imported with increasing frequency.

Match the relative size of your nano-reef with the maximum size of each species to determine which ones are suitable for your setup. Wrasses that reach 4 to 5 inches TL belong in aquaria no less than 15 gallons (56.85 l). Smaller specimens may be kept in aquaria larger than 7 gallons (26.53 l); smaller aquaria tend to not have sufficient space for even the smaller wrasses. In addition, most of the dwarf wrasses prefer 1 inch (2.5 cm) or more of a sandy substrate, such as sugar-sized aragonite, on the bottom of their aquarium in which to hide at night and during periods of stress. They also have a tendency to jump out of uncovered aquaria, further strengthening the case to keep a cover of some sort in place at all times.

DWARF SEABASSES AND REEF BASSLETS / FAMILY SERRANIDAE

Dwarf seabasses and **reef basslets** belong to the grouper family. Though many members of the family can grow to over 6 inches TL (15.5 cm), there are those that do not exceed 5 inches (12.5 cm) TL. These fishes generally happen to be very colorful and relatively mild mannered, and many are readily available in the aquarium hobby and hence affordable. They share similar care requirements with their distant cousins, the grammas and pseudochromids, meaning that adequate shelter and daily

The chalk bass (Serranus tortugarum) is a perfect resident for most nano-reef aquaria.

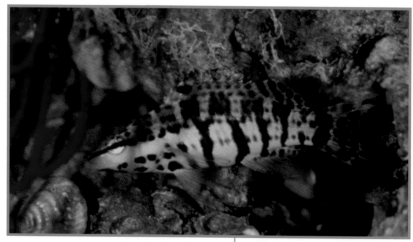

Another popular basslet is the harlequin bass (S. tigrinus).

feeding are necessary for long-term survival in captivity.

Dwarf seabasses of the genus *Serranus* hail from the tropical Atlantic. Three species that remain small enough to be housed in nano-reef aquaria are commonly seen in stores: the lantern bass (*Serranus baldwini*), harlequin bass (*S. tigrinus*), and chalk bass (*S. tortugarum*). Other less commonly seen but suitable species are the orangeback bass (*S. annularis*), twospot bass (*S. flaviventris*), and belted sandfish (*S. subligarius*). All are easily fed and disease resistant, and will not bother sessile invertebrates, though a few have been known to eat ornamental shrimp and smaller fish tankmates. They are related to groupers, after all!

Reef basslets are similar in appearance to dwarf seabasses, but they are far more colorful. Of the 23 or so described species, only one species is seen with any regularity in US stores: the Swissguard basslet. Other species such as the candy basslet (*Liopropoma carmabi*) and Swalesi reef basslet (*L. swalesi*) are occasionally offered, commanding a premium price. With only two exceptions[3], members of this family make outstanding nano-reef residents.

GRAMMAS / FAMILY GRAMMATIDAE

Grammas hail from the Western Atlantic and are very similar to the reef basslets—small in size, rarely growing over 3 inches (7.5 cm) in length, and quite colorful. One species, the royal gramma (*Gramma loreto*), is commonly seen in dealers' aquaria and is quite hardy, even-tempered, and affordable. Two additional members of the family are available on a less frequent basis—the Brazilian gramma (*G. brasiliensis*) and black-cap gramma (*G. melacara*).

Most members of the species are relatively mild-mannered (particularly when compared to the dottybacks), leaving most tankmates too large to swallow alone. Those not fitting that description may become a meal, however, so select tankmates accordingly.

The black-cap gramma (Gramma melacara) *makes for a beautiful addition to the nano-reef aquarium. This species is also referred to as the black-cap basslet.*

PSEUDOCHROMIDS / FAMILY PSEUDOCHROMIDAE

The behavior, feeding tendencies, approximate size when fully grown, and brilliant coloration of the **pseudochromids** make them the Pacific analogs of the grammas and justifiably earn many members of the family a well-deserved place in nano-reef aquaria. Though there are far more members in the family Pseudochromidae than in the family Grammatidae, they occupy the same niche as do the grammas, spending their time feeding on plankton drifting by in the currents, surveying their territory for small invertebrates and fishes, and chasing intruders away.

Pseudochromids suitable for housing in nano-reefs are among the smaller members of the family, attaining a length of no more than 5 inches (12.5 cm). It would be pointless to use demeanor as a qualification for this family, because nearly every member shows a tendency toward aggressive behavior, with some behaving brutally toward their tankmates. Interestingly, some of the smaller species are also the most aggressive! Each member of the family possesses very sharp teeth; combined with the unforgiving disposition of many pseudochromids, an encroaching fish with similar coloration is likely to be attacked, regardless of species, sex, or even size in some cases. (A few pseudochromids

Pseudochromis porphyreus, *or the magenta dottyback, can be found for sale in most aquarium shops.*

are noted to have attacked divers.) Particularly aggressive species are noted to be the oblique-lined dottyback (*Cypho purpurascens*), red dottyback (*Labracinus cyclopthalmus*), jaguar dottyback (*Pseudochromis moorei*), and Australian dottyback (*Ogilbyina novaehollandiae*). On the other end of the spectrum, the splendid dottyback (*Manonichthys splendens*), strawberry dottyback (*Pictichromis porphyrea*), bluelined dottyback (*Pseudochromis cyanotaenia*), orchid dottyback (*P. fridmani*), Sankey's dottyback (*P. sankeyi*), and Springer's dottyback (*P. springeri*) make up a short list of "less aggressive" species, generally speaking. The remaining species (there are 85 identified species in the family) fall somewhere in the middle.

As a general safety measure, when housing most members of this family in a nano-reef, it is wise to keep them in the absence of all other fishes and ornamental shrimp. The beauty and intriguing behavior of this family makes the sacrifice justifiable for pseudochromid enthusiasts. Exceptions to this approach are keeping a confirmed pair of conspecifics together for the purpose of breeding. Springer's dottyback and the orchid dottyback have been successfully spawned in small aquaria, and they make the best candidates for attempting this in a nano-reef of at least 15 gallons (56.85 l). While Sankey's dottyback appears to enjoy the presence of a small group of conspecifics, it is unlikely that any nano-reef is capable of maintaining a group for a lengthy period of time; therefore, keep them singularly if a confirmed pair is not available. The rest of the pseudochromids that are prone to spawning in captivity are best left to hobbyists with aquaria in excess of 30 gallons (113.7 l) total volume.

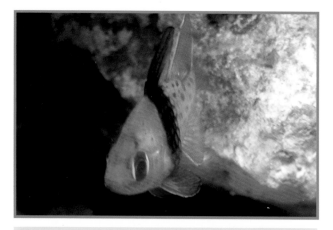

The polka-dot cardinalfish (Sphaeramia nematoptera) *does well when kept in small groups of three or more. These fish have large mouths and may feed on small motile inverts occasionally.*

CARDINALFISHES / FAMILY APOGONIDAE

The **cardinalfishes** are a group of small reef dwellers, most growing no larger than 3 inches TL (7.5 cm). They are hardy, disease resistant, accept most aquarium fare with gusto, and ignore invertebrates too large to be swallowed, making them ideal reef aquarium residents. Many species are nocturnal by nature, but they will eventually adapt to activity during daytime hours as long as an overhang that blocks direct light is present somewhere in the aquarium. These darker places in the aquarium enable the fish to shield their eyes and remain inconspicuous.

Of the many species that make up this family, only a few are available with any regularity in the U.S. aquarium market. Fortunately, several of them are nano-reef compatible. A few notable species are the orangestriped cardinalfish (*Apogon cyanosoma*), bluestreak or threadfin cardinalfish (*A. leptacanthus*), Banggai cardinalfish (*Pterapogon kauderni*), and pajama cardinalfish (*Sphaeramia nematoptera*). If purchased when small, flamefish (*Apogon maculates*) and members of the group displaying dark longitudinal stripes (*A.* spp.) may also be housed in these aquaria. Essentially, any member of the family that attains a maximum length of no more than 4 inches (10 cm) will make a good nano-reef resident.

Members of this family exhibit different levels of aggression toward other fishes as well as conspecifics. Some species noted for schooling will do little more than nudge each other to display their social dominance; however, once they've formed a breeding pair, the aggression becomes a bit more intense. In small aquaria (under 50–75 gallons [189.5–284.25 l], depending on the disposition of the species in question), solitary species will battle among themselves until only one fish from an initial group remains alive. The only reliable way to create a male-female pair with most members of the family[4] is to place a group of conspecifics in the same aquarium and let them get together. However, in the confines of even the largest

The Banggai cardinalfish (Pterapogon kauderni) *is another popular species of cardinalfish.*

nano-reef, this may not be feasible. Water quality might not be stable with so many fish in the system, and the aquarium is not large enough to allow sufficient hiding for ostracized individuals (who will take a beating from the pair). For these reasons, unless you know with certainty that you're obtaining a male-female pair, it is recommended that members of the family be housed as individuals in nano-reef aquaria. Species that naturally school can be reclusive when housed in this fashion, but when housed with other non-aggressive species, they often spend more time in plain view as their comfort level grows.

Dwarf seabasses, reef basslets, grammas, dottybacks, and cardinalfishes feed primarily on zooplankton, small fishes, worms, and crustaceans. The nutritional attributes of these foods are thought to play a major role in maintaining the intensity of the fish's coloration. Therefore, it is recommended that they receive a varied diet in captivity, containing foods rich in natural pigments such as canthaxanthin and astaxanthin. Members of these families leave all manner of sessile invertebrates alone, and notwithstanding the aggressive nature of some species toward piscine tankmates, are all great additions to nano-reef aquaria.

DAMSELFISHES / FAMILY POMACENTRIDAE

For many years, **damselfishes** have been a mainstay in the marine aquarium hobby, owing largely to their durability, bold coloration, availability, and affordability. Most species retail for a few dollars each, making them as affordable as many species of freshwater fishes. Damselfishes are not only attractive, but they are fascinating to observe. In terms of behavioral interaction,

This gorgeous little damsel is sometimes referred to as the flametail blue damsel.

damselfishes have probably been researched more than any other tropical reef fish. Many species actually "speak" to each other through a language of chirps, warning conspecifics to keep out of territorial boundaries and advertising for potential mates. As long as certain aspects of their behavior are taken into consideration, damselfishes can be very good nano-reef residents.

This well-known photo shows a group of tomato clowns (Amphiprion frenatum) *swimming among a sea of rose anemones. The large red coral in the middle is a* Dendronephthya *species.*

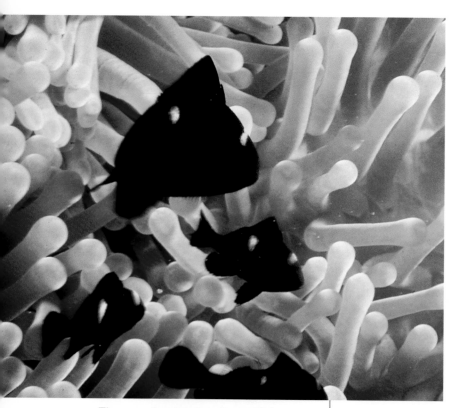

The popular domino damselfish
(Dascyllus trimaculatus) *grows large
and increasingly aggressive with age,
making its placement in a nano-reef a
temporary one at best.*

Members of this family display a wide array of coloration and obtain maximum sizes of approximately 2 inches (5 cm) to just over 12 inches TL (30 cm). As with the pseudochromids, many damselfishes exhibit a disproportionate amount of tenacity and aggression than their size would otherwise indicate, meaning that even a 2-inch (5-cm) damselfish can make life miserable for tankmates much larger in physical size. With the exception of the genus *Chromis*, which tends to be well behaved among all tankmates, pomacentrids are noted for their aggression and are therefore more suitable to be added to an aquarium last (or close to last, anyway)— certainly not first—if excessive (and potentially fatal) conflict is to be avoided. Additionally, it is not a good idea to place two conspecifics in the same aquarium; the more dominant fish will bully and likely kill the other fish. However, keeping more than two conspecifics in the same aquarium tends to lessen the hostility, as the most dominant fish must focus attention on multiple "intruders," and they on each other as well as the dominant fish (which is usually a large male). This approach is often successful, as long as all the fish remain alive. In my opinion, keeping more than one damselfish in all but the largest nano-reef aquaria is asking for trouble.

Numerous commonly available members of this family remain small enough for placement in nano-reef aquaria of 5 gallons (18.95 l) or greater total capacity. A few notable species are the blue damselfish (*Chrysiptera cyanea*), yellowtail blue damselfish (*C. parasema*), Talbot's damselfish (*C. talboti*), Fiji blue devil (*C. taupou*), three-striped damselfish (*Dascyllus aruatus*), four-striped damselfish (*D. melanurus*), Allen's damselfish (*Pomacentrus alleni*), neon damselfish (*P. coelestis*), princess damselfish (*P. vaiuli*), and yellowtail damoiselle (*Neopomacentrus azysron*). *Chromis* species tend to do best when housed with conspecifics, and even then the school should consist of more than three individuals to decrease squabbling and stress. They are also intolerant of wide fluctuations in water quality and poor water quality in general, making their placement in nano-reef aquaria a bit of a gamble.

Damselfishes have a misleading reputation for being able to tolerate poor water quality, and this has lead to countless fishes being used to help establish biological filtration in new aquarium setups. On this subject, there are a couple of points to take into consideration.

First, the family as a whole does not display this durability. In my experience, only members of the genus *Dascyllus* are as tolerant of poor conditions as is generally believed of the entire family; other species typically perish at some point during the cycle. Considering the number of "biological starter" products commonly available to marine aquarium hobbyists, as well as the fact that cured live rock can cycle an aquarium alone in a matter of days, needlessly exposing damselfishes (or any ornamental marine organism, for that matter) to these conditions is irresponsible and inhumane.

Also, as previously mentioned, it is prudent to add aggressive fishes to a new aquarium last, after the other fish in the aquarium have had a chance to establish a territory. Placing the most aggressive fish into the aquarium first will lead to confrontation and even the death of tankmates that are not capable of defending themselves against the certain onslaught they will face the first time the damselfish gets a look at them. Capturing a damselfish in a reef aquarium

The green chromis (Chromis atripectoralis) *does best when housed in groups. The problem is that a school of these fish needs more space than most nano-reefs can provide. Therefore, they may be better suited to larger marine aquariums.*

nearly always entails temporarily removing the majority of live rock and sessile invertebrates, which can be frustrating when you've spent so much time aquascaping the aquarium to look perfect.

All manner of invertebrates are largely ignored by damselfishes, another reason for their popularity among reef hobbyists. For those keeping nano-reef aquaria, the damselfishes have a lot to offer, as long as care is taken to place them with fishes of similar temperament.

ANEMONEFISHES / SUBFAMILY AMPHIPRIONIDAE

Anemonefishes are technically members of the damselfish family *Pomacentridae* and are probably the most widely recognized family of ornamental marine fishes in the United States, and perhaps the rest of the world. Upon seeing the somewhat comical swimming motions and contrasting colors of anemonefish, many people are mystified for at least a few moments, some for a lifetime. They are truly an endearing family. In general, members of this family make amiable nano-reef inhabitants, leaving all manner of invertebrates alone and preferring to remain near a host anemone or acceptable surrogate when no anemone is present.

Anemonefishes remain a manageable size in all but the smallest aquaria; adult females of most species may attain a length of 5 inches TL (12.5 cm), though 3 inches TL (7.5 cm) is closer to the norm. The family can be divided into six groups, with members of each group possessing similar physical and behavioral characteristics. They are:

- **The Tomato Complex.** There are five species in this group, all tending toward the upper end of anemonefish aggression and physical size attained as adults. They are

Tomato Clown

Clarkii Clown

best housed individually in nano-reef aquaria greater than 10 gallons (37.9 l) in total capacity.

- **The Clarkii Complex.** There are 11 species in this group, all essentially even tempered and medium to large in size when fully grown (relative to other members of this family). They may be housed individually in nano-reef aquaria greater than 7 gallons (26.5 l) total capacity. As a pair, a 15- to 16-gallon (56.8-to 60.6-l)nano-reef *might* be large enough quarters to keep the water parameters stable, but I recommend that they be placed in an aquarium no smaller than 20 gallons (75.7 l) for long-term care.

- **The Saddleback Complex.** There are three species in this group, none of them particularly common in the U.S. market. (See comments for the clarkii complex for characteristics and housing recommendations.)

- **The Percula Complex.** There are two species in this group, the "poster children" for the family. They remain relatively small in comparison to the aforementioned groups and may be housed individually in nano-reef aquaria greater than 7 gallons (26.5 l) total capacity, with a large nano-reef providing ample room for a pair.

- **The Skunk Complex.** There are six species in this group. All are relatively small, like members of the percula complex. However, unlike those fishes, skunk anemonefishes tend to be shy or exhibit nervous behavior. They may be housed in a like manner as members of the percula complex.

- **The Maroon Complex.** This "group" is composed of

Saddleback Clown

False Percula Clown

Skunk Clown

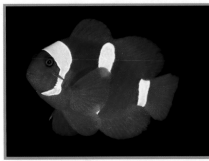
Maroon Clown

Livestock

103

PART TWO

> ### A Nano-Note on Anemonefishes
>
> **An interesting aspect of anemonefishes is the fact that they have been bred, both commercially and by hobbyists, since the late 1970s.**

one species, the maroon anemonefish (*Premnas bimaculatus*). This is a bold and aggressive species in which there is a marked difference in size between males and females. Generally, it is recommended that maroons be housed in a similar fashion as those within the tomato complex. Unless they are paired before being placed into the same aquarium, a female is almost assured of killing a male if both are added to even the largest nano-reef.

Also known as clownfishes, anemonefishes have gained much of their popularity through close interactions with sea anemones, which kill and eat all manner of fishes and invertebrates straying close enough to be stung with their tentacles, but which (depending upon the species of anemone) do not do so to anemonefishes. It was once widely held that the relationship between the anemonefish and its "host" anemone was symbiotic, meaning that the fish and the anemone could only survive in the presence of each other. The idea is that the anemonefish offers protection to the anemone against would-be predators and vice versa, and in some cases this may be true. One flaw with this notion is that, in nature, anemones are often seen without anemonefishes. However, anemonefishes are never seen without host anemones. An anemonefish without a host anemone will not survive long, owing to the fact that, without an anemone's protection, it is a pretty easy meal for a reef predator. By the same token, "vacant" anemones may be more susceptible to predation from species of fish that can wipe out entire anemone colonies. In light of this, more recent thought on the subject states that the relationship is actually mutualistic; that is, both the anemone and its anemonefish occupants gain some benefit from the association, specifically defense from predation. Note that in a reef aquarium, due to the general absence of anemone-eating fishes, it is possible to keep anemones without anemonefish companionship, and vice versa in an aquarium devoid of large piscivores.

Do not get the idea that all members of this family are passive. Although they generally exhibit a much calmer demeanor than do their scrappy damselfish cousins, maroon anemonefish (*Premnas bimaculatus*) and the species making up the tomato complex can be ferocious when it comes to encounters with other aquarium inhabitants, going so far as to attack the hands of the hobbyist from time to time during routine maintenance. Anemonefishes are generally compatible with others of their own species if they are introduced into the aquarium simultaneously, as long as the fish are either all juveniles or a male and female. The females of nearly all species grow much larger than males[5], so picking the female out of a tank of fish that are the same age is easy—simply pick the largest one in the group.

Pairing one large and one small fish nearly always results with a female and male, respectively, though if you're planning to breed these fishes, you should obtain the two fish from completely different sources to ensure genetic viability of the brood stock. It is a mistake to place two conspecific females in the same aquarium, as a battle will ensue with one loser (i.e., dead fish) being the result. Most anemonefish of different species get along well with each other, provided there are enough territories to go around, and in this regard it is always a good idea to have one or two more territories available than are needed, minimizing (but not necessarily eliminating) the chances of a territorial squabble. Unfortunately, providing sufficient accommodations for more than one species of anemonefish in a nano-reef is practically impossible, so keeping only one species per nano-reef is best.

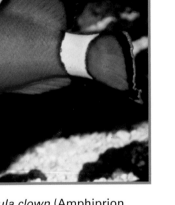

The true percula clown (Amphiprion percula) *is not as common as the false percula clown* (A. ocellaris), *but many think it is far more beautiful.*

Like many reef fish families, anemonefishes are hermaphrodites, meaning that they are able to undergo a reversal of sex at some point in their lives, conditions permitting. Members of this family are all born males, with the most dominant individual in a group undergoing a change to become a female when no other female is present. This sex reversal is known as **protandrous hermaphroditism**. The next most dominant fish in the group becomes a sexually mature male, and the rest of the males remain sexually inactive until there is a vacancy higher up the social ladder. Getting them to reproduce isn't too difficult, provided they have comfortable surroundings and the right food.

As previously stated, it is not necessary to keep an anemone for the anemonefish, and considering the difficulty in long-term care of captive anemones even in the largest aquaria with intense lighting and continual maintenance of proper water parameters, it seems a very bad idea to attempt keeping an anemone in a nano-reef. It is understood that there will be those hobbyists who want to attempt this, however, so please consider the following information carefully before you make a final decision and purchase:

- Consult a book on the captive care of host anemones and read it thoroughly. Then be sure that your system meets every single requirement of an anemone *before* you purchase an animal.
- Match the species of anemonefish you intend to keep with an appropriate host anemone. Note that not every species of anemone will host anemonefish!
- Anemones that have been recently purchased often prove difficult to place because they don't want to attach themselves to a rock or burrow into a crevice near the sand. This can be frustrating because anemones are essentially nothing more than bags of water, and current within the aquarium dislodges them easily before they can settle down in one spot.
- Recall the discussion on the tendency of anemones to wander. Anemones can be difficult to place in what you might consider an "ideal" location in the aquarium; rather, they may wander around the aquarium until they have found a location with ideal lighting and water flow characteristics, should that location exist.

It should be reiterated one more time that anemonefish do

Figure 6.1. Anemonefishes Known to Associate with the Bubble-Tip Anemone (*Entacmaea quadricolor*)

Amphiprion akindynos
A. allardi
A. bicinctus
A. chrysopterus
A. clarkii
A. ephippium
A. frenatus
A. mccullochi
A. melanopus
A. ocellaris
A. omanensis
A. rubrocinctus
A. tricinctus
Premnas biaculeatus

not need to be kept with a host anemone in captivity, particularly within the confines of a nano-reef aquarium in which the selection of tankmates should be limited to species of similar temperament. While the desire to house an anemonefish and anemone together in a nano-reef aquarium is understandable, you will experience less difficulty and greater success when providing a surrogate for the anemone, such as a small colony of *Rhodactis* sp. mushroom polyps.

GOBIES / FAMILY GOBIIDAE

Gobies are a rather diverse group of fishes exhibiting a range of shapes, sizes, color patterns, and feeding behaviors. They are one of the few families of ornamental fishes that are represented in marine, brackish, and freshwater environments.

The yellow watchman goby (Cryptocentrus cinctus) is probably the most common and easily recognized species of goby available to hobbyists.

Few members of this family spend much time actively swimming more than a few inches (centimeters) out in open water; instead, they are usually perched on or remain near a surface that enables them to feed and rest as desired. The primary reason for this behavior is the absence of a swim bladder, which prevents the fish from gaining neutral buoyancy in the water and causes them to sink when they stop swimming. These fishes typically spend the day on the lookout for food, which may be plankton, minute invertebrates living on the live rock within their territory, algae, or in the case of sand-sifting species, organisms living within the uppermost layer of sand around the base of the reef.

Numerous species exhibit characteristics that make them good nano-reef residents: remaining a manageable size, ignoring nearly all invertebrates, and being relatively even tempered. The so-called "shrimp gobies" of the genus *Amblyeleotris*, which includes such commonly available species as the orangespotted shrimp goby (*A. guttata*), Randall's shrimp goby (*A. randalli*), and Wheeler's shrimp goby (*A. wheeleri*); the watchman gobies of the genus *Cryptocentrus*, such as the yellow watchman goby

(*C. cinctus*) and pinkspotted shrimp goby (*C. leptocephalus*); and the identified members of the genus *Stonogobiops*, such as the blackray or barberpole shrimp goby (*S. nematodes*) and whiteray shrimp goby (*Stonogobius.* sp.), form symbiotic relationships with various species of snapping shrimp in the wild. The unlikely pair lives together in a burrow that the shrimp excavate in the sand, usually at the base of a rock. Snapping shrimp have poor eyesight, so they rely upon the goby to keep a lookout for predators or intruders. The shrimp keep one or more antennae on the goby to telegraph signals as to what is going on "outside." If a predator should appear, the pair immediately retreats into the depths of the burrow. However, if potential prey (such as a small fish or crustacean) should appear, the shrimp waits until the prey is in range, and then it stuns (and sometimes kills) the animal by creating a very loud sound, created when the

Rainford's goby (Amblygobius rainfordi) *is a wonderful little species that is rarely aggressive toward other fishes.*

shrimp snaps its enlarged claw shut. Using this system, both the goby and the shrimp eat on a regular basis and avoid predation. Re-creating this relationship inside a nano-reef can be as simple as obtaining a previously paired shrimp and goby or obtaining the proper species separately and introducing them to the aquarium at the same time.

Rainford's goby (*Amblygobius rainfordi*) has already been identified as one of the most useful species to maintain in a nano-reef aquarium, owing largely to its sand-sifting and algae-grazing activities. It also happens to be a very attractive species. The twinspot or signal goby (*Signigobious biocellatus*) is another attractive and useful species that performs limited sand-sifting duties. The clown gobies, of which there are numerous species commonly available, are perfect nano-reef residents, remaining very small even as adults and exhibiting a variety of color patterns. The same can be said of the neon gobies, of which there are three species commonly seen in the US market: the neon goby (*Gobiosoma oceanops*), sharknose goby (*G. evelynae*), and yellowstriped neon goby (*Gobiosoma* sp.). The sleeper gobies of the genus *Valenciennea* and the remaining sand-sifting gobies of the genus *Amblygobius* all get too large and require too much food for long-term nano-reef residency and should be placed in larger aquaria.

*Randall's shrimp goby (*Amblyeleotris randalli*) is one of the more spectacular gobies suitable for nano-reefs.*

Except in spacious aquaria, most members of the family do not get along well with conspecifics unless they are a mated pair, which means that they are best maintained singly in the confines of a nano-reef. Gobies are unlikely to harass invertebrates, aside from sand-sifting or burrowing species inadvertently dropping bits of sand or gravel on the bottom of the aquarium during feeding activities or excavation. Be vigilant in the removal from your aquarium of crabs and shrimp noted for preying upon gobies and other fish with similar swimming habits.

Gobies are often confused with blennies, and to the untrained eye it is easy to see why. Gobies and blennies share some physical similarities. One key difference between the two families is that gobies' pelvic fins are fused into a sort of suction cup, enabling them to adhere to surfaces regardless of position. Blennies, on the other hand, have no such modification. Also, most gobies have two separate dorsal fins, a spinous primary fin followed by a soft-rayed secondary, whereas blennies typically have one flowing dorsal fin.

DARTFISHES / FAMILY MICRODESMIDAE

Dartfishes are a small family closely related to the gobies, as is evident by their physical appearance. They are usually found in association with the reef face, where they spend their time

The firefish (Nemateleotris magnifica) *is a perfect addition to a nano-reef aquarium. Just be sure that these fish are not kept in the presence of other dartfishes, as they can be brutally aggressive toward one another.*

hovering in the water column in wait of food items carried by currents rather than resting on a surface as their goby cousins do.

There are three members of this family commonly encountered in the US market that fit the criteria for nano-reef residency: the purple firefish (*Nemateleotris decora*), firefish (*N. magnifica*), and Helfrich's firefish (*N. helfrichi*). These species remain relatively small, have a passive disposition, and bright coloration. Of the three, Helfrich's firefish is easily the most colorful and also the most expensive due to the rarity of its collection. It is not uncommon to see them in retailers' aquaria with a price tag of a couple hundred dollars.

Thankfully, the two remaining species are also brightly colored and affordable (at roughly $^1/_{10}$ the price of their gaudy cousin). These species always remain near a "bolt hole," a small cave or crevice in the reef into which they dart (appropriately) at the first threat of danger, and where they remain until the danger has passed. So strong is the instinct to remain in their hole, however, that dartfishes have reportedly been killed and eaten in them by large bristleworms, hermit crabs, emerald crabs, and mantis shrimp. Therefore, be wary of the motile invertebrates you choose to keep with these fish. Members of the family are somewhat timid and best suited to a reef aquarium with fishes of a similar temperament. The remaining members of this family require more swimming space than the confines of a nano-reef will afford.

This is the purple firefish, another suitable addition to nano-reef aquaria.

As with gobies, dartfishes don't readily appreciate the presence of conspecifics in close quarters, unless you can obtain a mated pair. It is therefore recommended that they be maintained singly in the nano-reef.

DRAGONETS / FAMILY CALLIONYMIDAE

Dragonets are a small family of fishes that are more familiar to many hobbyists by their alternate common names of mandarinfishes or scooter blennies. They are all associated with some sort of substrate, be it sand or rock, and reef-building invertebrates, from which they obtain their food.

The spotted mandarinfish (Synchiropus picturatus) is also known as the psychedelic mandarinfish. This beautiful species can be difficult to keep in nano-reefs unless an ample supply of microinvertebrates is available for them to feed on.

Four members of the family are commonly encountered in the US market. They are the spectacularly colored green or blue mandarinfish (*Synchiropus splendidus*), spotted mandarinfish (*S. picturatus*), scooter blenny or dragonet (*S. ocellatus*), and stellate dragonet or red scooter blenny (*S. stellatus*). Neither of the latter two species is a blenny, of course, which has led to confusion in their taxonomy among hobbyists for years.

None of these species grows very large, with 3.5 inches (8 cm) in length representing a truly giant specimen. Dragonets with drab coloration tend to be benthic (bottom dwelling), their brown mottled coloration camouflaging them effectively with the sand at the base of the reef. They spend their waking hours moving an inch or two at a time over the substrate, tirelessly searching for minute crustaceans upon which to feed. When startled or sleeping, these fishes dig themselves into the sand so that only a portion of their head is visible.

Blue and spotted mandarinfishes have few equals on the reef when it comes to coloration and pattern; their somewhat gaudy display serves to provide camouflage with the reef rubble and also warns

Mandarinfishes, such as the blue mandarinfish (Synchiropus splendidus) shown here, are best housed in large aquaria with ample live rock over which to browse, and in the absence of more active fishes (such as the sixline wrasse) sharing their dietary preferences. Mandarinfishes housed in nano-reef aquaria do not often survive longer than a few weeks or months, which is not an impressive time span.

potential predators of their slime coating, which is toxic to other fishes. A great service that mandarinfishes perform is the eradication of flatworms and planarians that sometimes find their way into reef aquaria and multiply so rapidly that they smother sessile invertebrates. Mandarinfishes placed into such settings immediately and happily go to work removing as many pests as they can find.

Members of this family are very intolerant of conspecifics in close proximity, unless the other fish happens to be of the opposite sex. A pair of dragonets would be hard pressed to find adequate food for long-term survival in an established reef aquarium under 75 gallons (284 l) in total capacity (and even then it would be a gamble), meaning that they should be housed singly in nano-reef aquaria.

Due to their meticulous feeding habits and the difficulty with which they are weaned onto dead foods, dragonets are largely incapable of outcompeting other fishes for prey. When housed with more active species that share their preferences for prey items, such as the sixline wrasse and its relatives, dragonets may die only a few weeks after they are purchased. The other main cause of their demise is being placed in a reef that does not have the food resources required for their survival. The fish can't find enough food to keep them healthy, and they weaken to the point that they succumb to a secondary infection or simply die of starvation. Because of these reasons, dragonets are best housed in a reef aquarium full of established live rock in which there are no competitors for their food source. They are also best housed with an attached refugium in which amphipods and other prey items may reproduce freely, maintaining a constant source of food for these fishes.

Trying to feed dragonets prepared foods used to be nearly pointless, as they would largely ignore anything drifting by in the water column. Recently, a small cyclops-like food has entered the market, and dealers and retailers have been having great success feeding and even fattening up emaciated dragonets with this product. Regardless, it is still strongly suggested that dragonets be excluded from reef aquaria unless they are mature and have a healthy population of the tiny invertebrates that these fishes feed on in the wild.

BLENNIES / FAMILY BLENNIIDAE

Blennies are one of the most interesting families of fishes to adorn reef aquaria. They feature a relatively small size, resistance to disease, a unique appearance (such as the presence of "eyelashes" or large lips), and a variety of behaviors that keep observers entertained. Like gobies, blennies lack a functional swim bladder and so sink when not actively swimming. Many species are sedentary, moving from perch to perch and resting only long enough to locate the next morsel of food, which may be algae, the polyps of stony corals (both large- and small-polyped varieties), and/or minute benthic invertebrates. Others swim in mid-water looking for plankton and small animals dislodged from their homes by the current or utilize stealth and mimicry to take bites out of fishes waiting to be cleaned by cleaner wrasses. Taking all of this into account, it becomes evident that thoroughly researching the feeding habits of any blenny you're interested in, regardless of the type of aquarium in which it is to be housed, is of paramount importance.

There are only a handful of commonly seen species in this family that can be comfortably and safely housed within the confines of a nano-reef, regardless of how large it is. Because some species may bite the polyps of stony corals and mantles of tridacnid clams and scallops, it is recommended that the following blennies be housed only in aquaria devoid of these invertebrates: the bicolor blenny (*Ecsenius bicolor*), red sea mimic blenny (*E. gravieri*), Midas blenny (*E. midas*), redlip blenny (*Ophioblennius atlanticus*), and seaweed blenny (*Parablennius marmorius*). The various fang blennies (genus *Meiacanthus*) may be housed in established nano-reefs with an abundant population of microinvertebrates upon which they will feed. (Again, a refugium attached to the nano-reef helps.) However, they will still

Keep an eye on blennies, as they can be bullies on smaller, more delicate fishes.

require frequent feeding that may make maintenance of water quality difficult. The lawnmower blenny (*Salarias fasciatus*) grows too large for long-term care in any nano-reef.

While not nearly as belligerent as some of the pseudochromids and damselfishes, blennies are noted for their assertive nature and can cause disarray in an aquarium housing delicate species. For this reason, choose tankmates capable of defending themselves against an occasional aggressive encounter. Delicate species such as firefishes are easily bullied by blennies and spend more time hiding than in the open, leading to starvation and illness.

SEAHORSES AND PIPEFISHES / FAMILY SYNGNATHIDAE

Seahorses and pipefishes are a group of fishes with a rather unusual appearance and special needs in captivity. Though they appear very different superficially, seahorses and pipefishes can be thought of as vertical and horizontal versions of each other. Many utilize cryptic shapes, colors, and textures of their skin to mimic marine plants, gorgonians, and the like. They are an endearing family, but one whose captive care should only be attempted by hobbyists willing to dedicate the time and resources to setting up a proper aquarium system and providing the proper types of food at the necessary densities. Failure to do so will result in the rapid demise of these delicate creatures. These animals should have an aquarium dedicated entirely to their care, rather than being placed into an already established system.

Seahorses can be difficult to care for in captivity, and this is mostly due to their unwillingness to feed on prepared foods. Thankfully, there are numerous species that are captive bred, and they seem to fare much better—even in nano-reefs!

Caulerpa *provides the seahorse keeper with a natural type of "hitching post" for their seahorses to anchor to.*

To begin with, the aquarium needs to have *very* modest water current, as neither seahorses nor pipefish are very strong swimmers. These fishes inhabit tidal lagoons, flat-bottomed seagrass beds, and other areas where the water current is normally very weak. This enables them to move about easily, swimming by moving their tiny dorsal and pectoral fins (seahorses) or dorsal and caudal fins (pipefishes). An aquarium with excessive laminar or turbulent water flow quickly weakens these fish, eventually leading to illness and/or death. By the same token, filter intakes should be completely covered with some porous material, such as reticulated foam, that prevents the fishes from inadvertently getting sucked in or stuck. Using air-driven water circulation (such as that used in a basic sponge filter) creates a very modest current that doesn't blow the seahorse or its prey around the aquarium, and there are no filter or pump intakes with which to be concerned.

Second, seahorses in particular spend most of their time entwined in seagrass blades or on the branches of gorgonians or some other such thin structure that allows them to gain a hold with their tail. Placing them into an aquarium devoid of these items, be they natural or otherwise, will do two things: First, it will force the seahorse to swim around aimlessly looking for an anchor point until it is exhausted, and second, it will take away the structures that seahorses use as camouflage when hunting for prey. Seahorses are able to blend in with their backgrounds to some extent[6]; this enables them to hunt with stealth, necessary when one considers their relatively feeble swimming abilities. Bearing all of this in mind, an adequate number of structures must be provided for the seahorses to utilize as anchor points and camouflage. Artificial plants with long blades, such as corkscrew *Vallisneria*, can be used to simulate sea grass. (The blades can be straightened by immersing them in hot water for a few seconds and then reshaping them.) Artificial gorgonians and sea whips are good anchors in reef tanks, as the constant rubbing of a seahorse's tail against the surface of a live gorgonian will strip and kill the tissue overlying the woody skeletal structure. If you are interested in housing these fishes with natural anchor points, consider the bare branches of dead gorgonians and small-polyped corals, or strap-bladed varieties of *Caulerpa* sp. macroalgae (where legal); *Caulerpa prolifera*, *C. mexicana*, and *C. seratuloides* make suitable anchor points. While these species of macroalgae perform a valuable service for the aquarium by removing dissolved organic materials and therefore promoting healthier water quality, remember that they will cause the pH in the system to fluctuate significantly from light to dark periods (the range tends to be particularly pronounced in small aquaria), and that they must have intense illumination to thrive. This last point is worth taking special note of—microalgae will grow on the bodies of seahorses, as they tend to be inactive swimmers.

Third, both seahorses and pipefishes are constantly on the lookout for food. Their diets consist largely of tiny crustaceans, fish larvae, and zooplankton, all of which are sucked into their slurp-gun-like mouths. In the aquarium setting, these fish require an almost constant supply of (preferably live) food, with prey items such as amphipods, brine shrimp, daphnia, copepods, and rotifers making up a varied and desirable diet. The trick is having the prey in significant densities in the aquarium to allow the fish to eat sufficiently, yet simultaneously avoiding an organic overload. One method that has been employed to release an essentially continuous flow of brine shrimp into an aquarium involves drilling a couple of small holes in the lid of a plastic container, such as a clean margarine tub, filling the container with water from the aquarium, adding a net full

The larger species of seahorses, such as this captive-produced Hippocampus *species, are best kept in aquaria larger than 10 gallons (38 l) in total volume.*

117

PART TWO   Livestock

of live brine shrimp, closing the container, and then placing it on the bottom of the aquarium near a weak current. (It might be necessary to weight the container with a rock.) Brine shrimp are attracted to light, and if the holes are small enough, only one shrimp will be able to exit each hole at any moment. In this fashion, the fish have a constant and more naturally presented supply of food. Feeding seahorses and pipefishes two times daily is typically sufficient for maintained health, although preparing them for breeding will require additional feedings.

Fourth, because of their slow swimming, these fish are easily out-competed by faster swimming fishes in terms of feeding. It is easy for seahorses to starve in an aquarium jammed with brine shrimp when tankmates are snatching up every morsel in sight. Therefore, tankmates should be limited to fishes that are not in competition for waterborne food (such as dragonets) and other syngnathids. By the same token, be very careful of invertebrate tankmates. Anemones and corals with long tentacles, as well as predatory crustaceans, will make easy meals of these weak swimmers.

At a mean 2 inches (5 cm), dwarf seahorses (Hippocampus zosterae) are gaining popularity, although they are among the most difficult to feed properly.

Seahorses and pipefishes are quite happy in each other's presence and seem to live longer if maintained in groups of three or more. One of the truly unique aspects of this family is that the males actually give birth to the young, the female doing nothing more than depositing the unfertilized eggs into the male's abdominal pouch. The male then fertilizes the eggs, and development of the larvae begins. When the young are fully developed, they leave the pouch as exact replicas of the adults, though tiny in size.

Unlike the aforementioned families in this chapter, some nano-reef aquaria might actually be too large to safely house some syngnathids. Dwarf seahorses, specifically, are best kept in aquaria no larger than 10 gallons (38 l) total capacity, and indeed smaller aquaria than that are preferred. A 2.5- or 3-gallon (9.5-to 11-l) nano-reef, properly outfitted, is actually large enough to house several of these diminutive creatures! By contrast, larger members of this family should be maintained in aquaria *larger* than 10 gallons (38 l) total capacity as a result of their larger appetites (leading to increased waste concentrations) and need for space to move about.

While some hobbyists might suggest keeping live sponges in seahorse aquaria to provide a place for the fish to attach, this practice is not advisable in a nano-reef. Sponges rely on food captured by filtering water through their cells for survival, and providing sufficient particulate food to keep sponges alive in such a small aquarium quickly leads to problems with water quality. By contrast, zoanthids can survive quite happily with nothing more than the light from an 18-watt power compact bulb and regular partial water changes. Incidental food items that they might catch during the course of each day will supplement their nutritional requirements.

This information is intended only as a general introduction to the family. If your interest lies in keeping seahorses or pipefishes in captivity, do as much research as you possibly can *before* you make any decisions about setting up the aquarium up or purchasing the livestock.

Feeding Fishes in the Nano-Reef Aquarium

One of the most crucial considerations to recognize prior to purchasing a new fish is the dietary requirement of the species. Unless you can provide the foods it will

The best choice of sessile invertebrates for a nano-reef housing syngnathids is zoanthids, of which there are so many varieties that a very pretty aquarium could easily be aquascaped with nothing else!

Livestock

119

PART TWO

need to thrive over the course of years, leave it alone and move on to another species that you are able to properly accommodate. I have received too many questions from hobbyists who have purchased a fish without knowing what it ate, only to discover that they had no means of feeding it successfully. This is a very irresponsible approach to being an aquarium hobbyist.

With the wide array of feeding requirements exhibited by marine fishes, a neophyte might think that he or she would need to allocate a shelf in the cupboard, fridge, or freezer solely to fish food. In reality, feeding is fairly straightforward and calls only for some common sense. The more dedicated an aquarium hobbyist you become, invariably the wider the variety of foods you will stock for your charges. Starting out, though, can be as simple as providing appropriate sources of protein, vegetable material, fatty acids, and vitamins.

The families that have been discussed in this chapter have, for the most part, easily met feeding requirements; exceptions are the dragonets and syngnathids, which require live food at least initially if they are to survive long enough to be weaned onto prepared or frozen food. Table 5.1 lists the families and their feeding preferences.

The families have been separated into general categories corresponding to their feeding requirements. To maintain long-term health and coloration, provide the most varied diet possible

Table 5.1. Feeding Chart for Nano-Reef-Compatible Families				
Family/Subfamily	Marine Algae	Marine Flesh	Zooplankton	Benthic Invertebrates
Dwarf Angelfishes	•	•	•	•
Damselfishes	•	•	•	•
Blennies	•	•	•	•
Gobies	•	•	•	•
Dwarf Seabasses and Reef Basslets		•	•	•
Grammas		•	•	•
Pseudochromids		•	•	•
Cardinalfishes		•	•	•
Wrasses		•	•	•
Anemonefishes		•	•	•
Dartfishes		•	•	
Dragonets			•	•
Sea Horses and Pipefishes			•	•

based on the requirements of that family. The coloration, in particular, of numerous species of reef fishes has a tendency to fade in captivity, and foods rich in natural pigments can prevent this from happening and may even reverse fading, given time.

MARINE ALGAE

Marine algae refers to various types of microalgae and macroalgae, and can also include dried kelp such as nori and dulse. Plant material is a very important part of the diets of many fishes because it provides important nutrients, as well as vitamins, that are not obtainable elsewhere. The growth of microalgae in a nano-reef will provide some of the vegetative matter required by those species given to grazing, but supplemental feeding of kelp or some food rich in marine algae is recommended.

MARINE FLESH

Marine flesh consists of raw squid, shrimp, clam, and the white meat of non-oily fishes (such as cod and flounder). It can be cut or chopped into tiny pieces and fed directly, or incorporated into a prepared food. Live feeder shrimp and the fry of livebearers are also appreciated by many representatives of the families in this section.

ZOOPLANKTON

Zooplankton, by definition, consists of animals that are at the mercy of the ocean's currents. That is a very broad description. For the purposes of the hobbyist, creatures such as copepods, brine shrimp (both nauplii and adults), daphnia, rotifers, and the larvae of cnidarians and crustaceans make up the category. While they may be fed in frozen form, you'll find that

Macroalgae are great for nutrient reduction in a nano-reef aquarium. However, they can grow out of control very quickly, so keep a close eye on them.

Livestock

121

PART TWO

livestock prefer these creatures alive and active. Dragonets and syngnathids, in particular, hunt by detecting their prey's movement; until they have become used to feeding on motionless prey, attempts to feed them with frozen or dead foods will largely be in vain. While the use of frozen or freeze-dried zooplankton might prolong the time before nutritional deficiency begins to severely impact the fishes' health, it should not be used as a complete substitute. Hatching brine shrimp is a very simple and educational process that builds further interest in the aquarium hobby, particularly among youngsters. Brine shrimp eggs and hatcheries are relatively inexpensive and available through various retailers and online suppliers. Daphnia, rotifers, and copepods require a bit more effort, but they are still worthwhile to culture at home. If you are interested in plankton culture, a good book on the subject is a worthy investment.

BENTHIC INVERTEBRATES

Benthic invertebrates are the tiny creatures you see on the live rock and live sand, mostly at night using a dim flashlight. Amphipods, copepods, tiny mollusks, and polychaete worms make up the bulk of this category. These organisms build in population density as an aquarium ages (due to the increasing abundance of organic material in the system), with predation from fishes keeping their numbers in check. If your intention is to house dragonets in a nano-reef and you'd prefer not to culture live plankton, it is imperative that there be a healthy population of benthic invertebrates in the system *before* introducing the fish to the aquarium. A refugium will help maintain this population by providing the creatures with a safe place to feed and reproduce. Far too many dragonets have perished from starvation because they were placed into immature reef aquaria.

Small invertebrates are the preferred foods of nearly all nano-reef inhabitants.

PELLET & FLAKE FOODS

Due to their availability and ease of use, pellet and flake foods are popular with many aquarium hobbyists. While it is common belief that these foods can degrade water quality when overfed, it is more correct to say that *any* food left to decay in the system would have this impact. The main benefit to using these types of foods is convenience; it doesn't get much easier than unscrewing the cap and placing a little food in the aquarium. Manufacturers of quality foods utilize a broad base of ingredients that can be relied upon to provide a large percentage of the fishes' nutritional needs. I recommend that these foods compose no more than 50% of the fishes' daily intake, however, to encourage a more varied diet that is only the result of feeding additional foods. Omnivorous fishes, such as those represented in the uppermost group in Table 5.1, will generally accept both pellet and flake foods with little reservation. Members of the middle group, being essentially carnivorous, are not as easy to convince of the palatability of these foods, although they may come to accept them with time. Members of the bottom-most group will rarely, if ever, accept these foods.

While prepared foods are an option for many hobbyists in general, it should be noted that they are not the first choice of many *advanced* hobbyists. Rather than open a can of pellets or flakes and feed the fish, they would prefer to provide a diet derived from fresh or frozen fish, shrimp, crab, squid, beef heart, the oils of marine fishes, sources of vegetation such as nori, laver, and dulse seaweed, and a blend of vitamins and fatty acids. Recipes for food preparations abound in popular literature and on the Internet, so if you are interested in creating such a diet for your fishes, there seems to be no end to the possibilities. My own

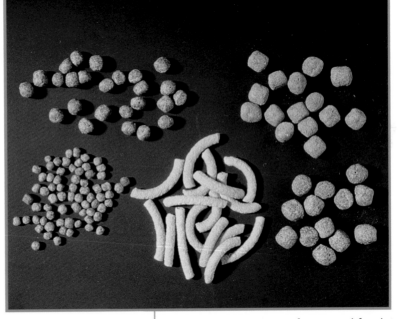

There are many types of prepared foods on the market. Be sure to examine as many of them as possible, not only for their contents but also to make sure that they are of the proper size for the fishes that you keep.

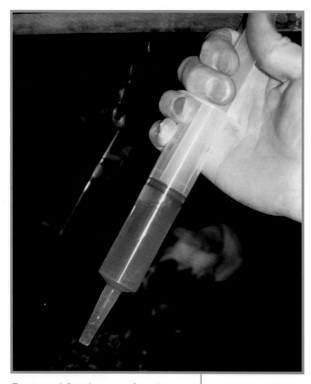

Prepared foods can often be fed to the inhabitants of your nano-reef through a syringe. This allows only a small amount of food to be released at a time and also allows it to be directed toward specific organisms.

preparation is usually made from combining:

- one 8-oz. cod filet (fresh)
- several sheets of nori
- 3–4 tbsp freeze-dried cyclops
- 10-ml multi-vitamin supplement
- 10-ml vitamin-C supplement
- 5-ml fish oil

Basically, I combine all of the ingredients in a food processor and blend until homogenous. Then, I place enough of the mixture in a storage bag to lay flat to a depth of no more than $1/4$ inch and freeze. To feed, break off small pieces and place in the aquarium, or shred with a grater into strips that the fishes and motile invertebrates can eat.

Of great importance in a nano-reef are the questions of how much to feed and how often, because overfeeding rapidly impacts water quality in such a small system. If you were to return to childhood and use Mr. Rogers as an example of feeding the fish, not only would you need to buy a new container of food every other day, but the aquarium would be so loaded with organic material that you would have a very hard time seeing the livestock amidst the muck, much less keeping them alive. One intelligent approach to effective feeding is to gauge what you think the fish will eat and then cut it in half. Feed the fish the first half of the food, wait several minutes for the food to be eaten, and then add a *portion* of the remaining food. Again, wait for the food to be eaten, and then determine if the fish still appear hungry. (i.e. Are they still searching for food? Have they settled down somewhere to rest? Did you notice them eating a few pieces of food and ignoring consequent pieces that came into their view? etc.) If in doubt, do not feed any more for that session. You would be amazed at how little food this really amounts to. Remember that in a reef aquarium, the feeding you perform is meant to *supplement* the diet of many species of fishes, not be the basis. Fish that do not receive enough to eat through their browsing will be very excited when feeding time arrives, and as long as you appear at the aquarium at the same times each day with food in hand, you will find the fish near the surface, awaiting the feast.

Most fishes in the wild are on the lookout for food constantly, and this behavior carries over to life in captivity. If food is present and the fish are hungry, they will eat it. The fishes deemed nano-reef compatible are best fed one or two times each day to help avoid the negative impact on water quality that a constant influx of organic material can have. Active swimmers must generally be fed more frequently than sedentary species, owing to the rate at which they expend calories. Two or three feedings each day is sufficient.

The African flameback pygmy angel (Centropyge acanthops) *is one of those fishes that will tirelessly search out food. Don't be tempted to offer them food too often though; feeding any more than 1-2 times per day may cause water quality problems in their tank.*

Chapter Six

Motile Invertebrates
for the Nano-Reef Aquarium

As seen earlier, the limited volume of water in a nano-reef sometimes makes keeping fishes a challenge. An option worth exploring is to stock such small aquaria with organisms that have more modest feeding and space requirements. **Motile invertebrates** can be vividly colored, fascinating to watch, able to withstand fluctuating water conditions, and easy to care for. The majority of them are inexpensive when compared to reef fishes, making them an attractive option for the nano-reef hobbyist on a tight budget. Additionally, many can be kept in even the smallest nano-reefs.

The selection of motile invertebrates available to hobbyists is quite large. The critical consideration when deciding which types to purchase is the compatibility of these creatures with the other animals that you wish to include in your collection. Motile invertebrates that have earned a reputation for catching and eating small fishes are poor choices for housing in nano-reef aquaria. For this reason, emerald and Sally Lightfoot crabs are excluded from the list of acceptable nano-reef species, which can be seen in Table 6.1.

Table 6.1. Non-Predatory Motile Invertebrates Compatible With Nano-Reef Aquaria.		
Feeding Behavior	**Common Name**	**Genus**
Browsers and Grazers	Snails	*Astraea*
		Margarites
		Trochus
		Turbo
	Limpets	*Diodora*
		Fissurella
	Abalone	*Haliotis*
	Paper Bubbles	*Bulla*
	Lettuce Slugs	*Tridachia*
	Hermit Crabs	*Calcinus*
		Clibanarius
		Paguristes
	Sea Urchins	*Arbacia*
		Mespilia
		Tripneustes
	Sea Stars	*Fromia*
Filter Feeders	Porcelain Anemone Crabs	*Neopetrolisthes*
Scavengers	Snails	*Cerithium*
		Nassarius
		Nerita
		Pusiostoma
	Shrimp	*Lysmata*
		Periclimenes
		Rhynchocinetes
		Saron
		Thor
Sand Sifters	Snails	*Cerithium*
		Nassarius
		Pusiostoma

Crustaceans, Gastropods, and Echinoderms

There are three main groups of motile invertebrates commonly available in the aquarium market—crustaceans, gastropods, and echinoderms. These groups can be subdivided into two broad groups (predators and non-predators) by their feeding behaviors—whether they are browsers, grazers, filter feeders, scavengers, sand sifters, or predators. While this may seem an overgeneralization of sorts, it serves the hobbyist's purposes in the relevance of nano-reef aquaria.

Brittle stars are important, and interesting, members of the reef community. Watch out though as they can be highly predatory on smaller animals.

A balanced reef environment contains representatives of all links in the food chain. A discussion on reef ecology is beyond the scope of this book, and at any rate, the hobbyist is maintaining "artificial systems" of sorts, so a complete balance is not necessary. It may, however, be stated that an aquarium replete with primary producers (plants and algae) through all levels of the consumer group (bacteria, microinvertebrates, and the successive organisms that live upon them and each other) tends to remain more stable in the long run than a system with an overabundance of one type of organism, largely because resident populations are held in check by predation and the availability of nutrients. In a nutshell, a balanced ecosystem makes for a stable reef aquarium, regardless of the volume.

It could be said that certain groups have a predisposition toward grazing, sand sifting, and so on. However, many motile invertebrates are omnivorous and opportunistic, meaning that they will feed on just about anything available or abundant. This is of benefit in a nano-reef particularly because a few "utility janitors" can do the jobs of several less flexible species.

CRUSTACEANS

Crustaceans are principally represented by crabs, shrimp, and lobsters. Barnacles, isopods, and amphipods are also members of the class. Crustaceans are probably the most popular group of motile invertebrates in the aquarium hobby. These organisms belong to the phylum Arthropoda, which also includes merostomates (horseshoe crabs) and pycnogonids (sea spiders), neither of which is likely to be a nano-reef resident.

GASTROPODS

The gastropods are members of the phylum Mollusca, which also includes the cephalopods (octopus and their allies), the bivalves (clams and other sedentary shellfish), and the polyplacophorans (chitons). Suitable gastropods for nano-reefs include snails, abalones, limpets,

Various forms of gastropods are available to nano-reefers for inclusion in their aquarium. After a while, coralline algae will begin to grow on their shells and they'll be hard to distinguish from the rock on which they crawl.

sea slugs, and sea hares. Cephalopods are largely unsuitable as nano-reef residents, owing to their size, feeding requirements and consequent waste production (which is too great for most filtration systems on nano-reef aquaria to effectively handle), nocturnal hunting habits, and penchant for escape from the aquarium itself. Limpets and chitons are incidental introductions to reef aquaria, coming in as stowaways on uncured live rock. They are not, to my knowledge, offered for sale separately. Three additional classes of organisms fall into this phylum, but they are not collected for the aquarium trade.

ECHINODERMS

Echinoderms are broadly represented by sea stars, brittle stars, sea urchins, and sea cucumbers. (Sand dollars and basket stars also belong to this phylum.) These organisms represent three separate classes within the phylum (*Stelleroidea*, *Echinoidea*, and *Holothuroidea*) and are often introduced into reef aquaria accidentally on live rock, both cured and uncured.

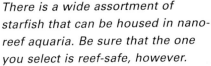

There is a wide assortment of starfish that can be housed in nano-reef aquaria. Be sure that the one you select is reef-safe, however.

Browsers and Grazers

Organisms that spend their waking hours in search of live plant material and microorganisms such as bacteria and protozoans are referred to as either browsers or grazers. This group is one of the most important links in the reef ecosystem and deserves a place in every nano-reef, regardless of volume. Most gastropods, sea urchins, and hermit crabs available to hobbyists act in this capacity.

The key to striking a balance with the number of these janitors in a reef aquarium is to keep only as many as can keep the natural growth of algae and diatoms cropped. If there are too many of these animals in a reef, supplemental feeding is required, which amounts to placing dried seaweed or a vegetable such as romaine lettuce, spinach, or broccoli in the aquarium. It should be cautioned, however, that some grazers have messy eating habits and clip off large pieces of food, which then float around the aquarium until they get pulled into a pump or filter intake or wind up in some inaccessible area of the reef where they eventually decompose. It is for this reason that supplemental feeding of grazers is best avoided in a nano-reef, as the potential associated impact on water quality can make life temporarily difficult for the livestock and hence the hobbyist. It is far simpler to limit the number of grazers in the aquarium from the onset to no more than one per pound ($^1/_2$ kilogram) of live rock used in the reef.

Sea urchins are very interesting creatures to house in a nano-reef. However, they tend to knock corals and rocks over, so watch them carefully.

Table 6.1 (on page 128) lists only two varieties of sea urchins as being nano-reef compatible. The reason that other types have been omitted is that they tend to grow too large for long-term housing in a nano-reef, where they would topple live rock and potentially damage sessile invertebrates with their movements. The Atlantic purple sea urchin (*Arbacia punctulata*) remains relatively small and is a common hitchhiker on uncured live rock. This species is a very effective grazer of filamentous algae and makes a great addition to a nano-reef over 7 gallons (26.5 l) in total capacity. Aquaria under that volume are best grazed by gastropods and hermit crabs, which remain relatively small and have fewer tendencies to topple rockwork, though their climbing activity sometimes dislodges sessile invertebrates.

Filter Feeders

Organisms that utilize special feeding appendages to strain the passing water are referred to as **filter feeders**. Generally, their food consists of plankton and tiny creatures that have been dislodged from the reef by strong currents. In stores, the only motile invertebrates that fit this description are likely to be the porcelain anemone crabs of the genus *Neopetrolisthes*. In the wild, these small crabs remain under the protection of a host anemone, an arrangement that should be replicated in an aquarium setting.

Brittle stars are noted filter feeders that also act in the capacity of scavengers in the reef aquarium. However, no species remain small enough for long-term housing in even the largest nano-reef. Several species of sea apples also strain food from the passing currents, but the species that are offered for individual sale are noted for producing toxins when irritated, which can quickly prove fatal to organisms living within the confines of a nano-reef. There are incidental introductions of tiny brittle stars and sea cucumbers with live rock that may remain small enough for such a small aquarium, however, if you're lucky enough to have a few sneak in as stowaways.

Sea apples are very colorful members of the class Holothuroidia, which includes other sea cucumbers. While they are beautiful, they are also potentially deadly to most, if not all, marine aquarium inhabitants should they eject their internal organs or become sucked into an aquarium pump inlet; a toxin is released that can quickly make a graveyard of any aquarium. In the author's opinion, such organisms should be omitted from all aquaria with the exception of those cared for by hobbyists that understand how to set up the proper aquarium and know the consequences involved with keeping the creatures.

Scavengers and Sand Sifters

These organisms feed largely upon decaying plant and animal material. In nature, scavengers are considered to be extremely important, because they facilitate the recycling of nutrients from complex to basic forms so that the cycle of life can proceed uninhibited. Sand-sifting motile invertebrates literally burrow through the sand, consuming organic material as they go. They are of extreme importance in all marine aquaria with a bed of live sand, because they help prevent the buildup of latent organic material that leads to hydrogen sulfide production and poor water quality.

All reef aquaria should have scavengers of some description, and as previously mentioned, this isn't too hard to accomplish given the omnivorous nature of most sessile invertebrates. Nonetheless, there are those that live predominantly in this fashion, with several being nano-reef compatible. There will be times when insufficient food exists for organisms that are primarily scavengers, and this can lead to their starvation or indiscriminate feeding on other invertebrates. Avoid this situation by housing no more than one scavenger per 3 gallons (11.37 l) of total capacity in the nano-reef, and feed these creatures once each week with a small piece of fish or squid placed in the aquarium a couple of hours after the lights have turned off for the evening.

Sand-sifting duties in a nano-reef tend to be best performed by snails. While sea cucumbers are the undisputed masters of cleaning substrate (by eating it, digesting the organic material within the sediment, and then passing it out their back ends), most of these organisms grow far too large for housing in a nano-reef. Those that do not are noted for producing toxins when irritated. In the

While not exceptionally beautiful, sea cucumbers are masters of sand sifting and detritus removal.

confines of a nano-reef, such an event stands a very good chance of being catastrophic to the lives of all aquarium inhabitants.

The following is a list of what are considered to be the most effective all-around janitors for nano-reef inclusion:

- **Scavengers and Sand Sifters:** Snails of the genus *Cerithium*. These snails are most noted for scavenging and burrowing through the sand. While there are reports that they eat microalgae, other organisms have been found to be far more effective at grazing than these snails. In a pinch, they *could* be used as the sole janitorial staff in a nano-reef, though.

Snails are commonly used to remove algae growing on the glass and live rock in a nano-reef aquarium.

- **Grazers of Live Rock:** The scarlet reef hermit crab (*Paguristes cadenati*). These crabs are brightly colored and spend the majority of the day hard at work removing algae and organic material from live rock. They are also active, moving from location to location in search of "greener pastures."
- **Grazers on the Aquarium Viewing Surface:** The paper bubble (*Bulla* sp.). These interesting creatures are a type of gastropod that is somewhere between a snail and a nudibranch in morphology. Nocturnal in nature, these organisms are extremely effective grazers of microalgae, leaving macroalgae and all sessile invertebrates alone. They are also prolific, and many hobbyists report literally hundreds of progeny produced by just a few adults.

Another interesting note about these gastropods is that they move faster than any snail or sea slug commonly seen, with a particularly fast specimen covering a distance of several inches (centimeters) in only a few seconds. As with the other organisms in this list, paper bubbles will scavenge when opportunity arises.

Predators

Those organisms that hunt and prey upon non-plant organisms are basically predators. They are not limited to animals, for there are plants—and even microbes—that can be considered predatory. Predatory ornamental motile invertebrates are popular additions to marine aquaria (when they are introduced intentionally), but be aware that incidental introductions of these organisms can decimate the livestock and cause great frustration to unsuspecting hobbyists, especially newcomers to the hobby who may not know the telltale signs of their presence. Regardless, because of their highly predatory nature, they need frequent feedings of meaty foods, and that leads to an increase in waste production. A nano-reef should therefore house no more than one of these organisms, if for nothing more than the sake of minimizing the impact on water quality for the rest of the livestock in the system.

Several filter-feeding crabs, such as the one shown, are available to hobbyists and generally co-exist peacefully with other crustaceans and fishes.

The list of predatory motile invertebrates that remain small enough for inclusion in large nano-reef aquaria is limited to only a few species. If you are inclined to house one of these animals, they can be well worth the effort to obtain them.

MANTIS SHRIMP

These are one of nature's invertebrate marvels. Their appearance incorporates characteristics of a shrimp, lobster, and praying mantis (hence the name), their eyesight is among the sharpest in the entire animal kingdom, their intelligence is often astonishing, and the speed at which they dispatch their prey is the fastest recorded animal movement on earth. Large specimens are often captured by commercial fishermen and oceanographers during trawls along the sea floor, and these shrimp are left alone—because they have earned the nickname of "thumb splitters" due to their ability to slice a person's thumb wide open with their dagger-like appendages—to escape through the deck drains and back into the ocean. These are formidable creatures, but small specimens make fascinating aquarium residents.

Mantis shrimp are not really shrimp at all, though they are close relatives. They rely upon stealth, cunning, and a pair of spiked or clubbed arms to hunt their prey, which consists largely of other motile invertebrates

Mantis shrimps make fascinating nano-reef residents but generally require a dedicated aquarium free of other motile invertebrates or fishes; not following this recommendation will inevitably result in those organisms' becoming food for the shrimp. Nonetheless, mantis shrimp are highly intelligent as invertebrates go, being second perhaps only to cephalopods.

Only occasionally will you see a mantis shrimp actively swimming through the water. Most of the time they're hidden deep within the rocks.

and small fishes[1]. The arms are held in at the sides of the shrimp when at rest, and they are used to punch or impale their prey with lightning speed; the prey literally never sees the punch coming. In their natural setting, mantis shrimp occupy a burrow or cave in the sediment or rock, which they either excavate themselves or take from another organism (which they have typically eaten). The den, as it is called, always has two exits—one is for regular use, the other is to escape predators. This is one of the behavioral aspects of mantis shrimp that makes them so hard to extract from a reef aquarium; the only way to accomplish this task without removing every rock in the aquarium is to use a special trap. However, this approach isn't guaranteed to work, for the mantis will look at the trap from every possible vantage point before going anywhere near it, much less inside. These are bold, calculating creatures that become akin to a family pet as time goes by. A mantis that feels secure in its aquarium will greet you in the morning when the lights turn on and then spend a great deal of time in the open looking for food during the day.

A nano-reef stocked with various cnidarians makes a suitable home for mantis shrimp. The lower the density of the rock used, the better, as the shrimp is likely to either burrow beneath a rock or beat a hole in one for a den. Avoid placement of ornamental crustaceans of any sort, gastropods (with the exception of nocturnal varieties), sea urchins, and bivalves into this aquarium, unless they are meant to be prey.

If you need to clean the viewing surface of the aquarium thoroughly with a magnet or scraper, you need not be overly concerned about the shrimp attacking your hand because the only time they are likely to defend themselves is if they feel trapped. Hermit crabs—regardless of size—in such an aquarium are likely to vanish. Angelfishes and anemonefishes in a host anemone are generally safe from mantis shrimp. However, most hobbyists prefer to house these interesting invertebrates as the sole motile inhabitant in a nano-reef. Do not place more than one mantis shrimp into a nano-reef because these creatures are highly intolerant of each other's presence, and the result will be an intense fight with one clear victor.

During the first few weeks after introducing a mantis shrimp to an aquarium, its prey items should be live and moving. Feeder guppies and glass shrimp, both fortified with a good flake fish food beforehand (gut loaded) to increase their nutritional value, are perfect for this task. Feeding with one or two guppies or shrimp (depending upon their size) every three days is usually sufficient. If you find feeding live organisms to your shrimp distasteful, you can try to gradually switch its diet to pieces of fresh fish and shrimp. In this case, feed one piece of fish or shrimp, roughly $^1/_4$ inch square by $^1/_2$ inch thick, every three days.

The best places to obtain mantis shrimp for a nano-reef seem to be from collectors who work in South Florida and throughout the Caribbean. Most mantis shrimp collected in these areas are of the genus *Gonodactylus*, the so-called "clubbers" or "bashers" because of the swollen claws used to beat and kill their prey. These species range from olive to lime green or may be salmon to bright orange in coloration, and they generally remain under 3 inches (7.5 cm) or so in total length. They are captured as stowaways in pieces of live rock.

SNAPPING SHRIMP

Sometimes referred to as pistol shrimp, snapping shrimp are a group of true shrimp that have developed a weapon similar in effect to that of the mantis shrimp's arms—an oversized claw that, when shut, creates a sound so powerful that it stuns or kills prey within a close range. Although these shrimp often scavenge, they are much better classified as predators because the physiological development of their claw is certainly not a result of searching for decaying plant and animal tissue. This interesting group of crustaceans lives by a "wait here and let the world come to me" motto. They rarely venture outside their den to look for prey unless they feel particularly safe from predation.

Note the oversized claw on this shrimp—a sure sign that this is one type of "snapping" shrimp.

Searching for a new den typically happens at night under cover of darkness.

Snapping shrimp have relatively poor eyesight, which is one reason that you will commonly see them with a goby counterpart. The goby and the snapping shrimp will share a den together. This is highly beneficial to the shrimp because the goby can spot potential prey or predators much more quickly than the shrimp, enabling both to survive more easily. The goby obtains food from the organisms that the shrimp kills, and the shrimp avoids predators—a very unique symbiotic relationship.

Replicating this relationship within a nano-reef aquarium makes for a shrimp that is more comfortable with its surroundings and hence remains visible more than it would otherwise were no goby present. In fact, without a goby den mate, it is unlikely that you will see the shrimp very much at all.

Snapping shrimp often enter an aquarium unbeknownst to the hobbyist via new live rock additions. Their presence is given away by the occasional sound of their claw creating the characteristic popping sound (which has alarmed many an unsuspecting hobbyist into thinking that his or her aquarium was cracking). On rare occasions, this popping sound will be accompanied by the disappearance of a small fish in the aquarium. Truly bold (or hungry) snapping shrimp may target fish as large as a Banggai cardinalfish (*Pterapogon kauderni*) for a potential meal.

Housing these shrimp is the same as for mantis shrimp, the only difference being that gastropods are largely ignored by

A Nano-Note on Lobsters

I have chosen to exclude lobsters from the list of nano-reef-compatible motile invertebrates because they tend to require more feeding than the filtration on such a small aquarium can handle. Also, they spend most of the day hiding or are inactive; these attributes make for a less than desirable nano-reef resident, in my opinion. If you would like to house a lobster in your nano-reef, I suggest looking at the small reef lobsters of the genus *Enoplometopus*, which are colorful and remain relatively small. A particularly aggressive filtration system may be able to counter the waste produced by feeding, but they will still remain largely nocturnal.

snapping shrimp and are therefore usually safe in this setup. By the same token, bivalves are in little danger of being eaten. Hermit crabs, ornamental shrimp, and small fishes, on the other hand, are certainly at risk of becoming a meal for snapping shrimp should they wander within range of the shrimp's claw.

Snapping shrimp are available through most Indo-Pacific collectors, so aquarium stores and online retailers usually have access to a variety of species throughout the year. On occasion, a shrimp and goby that were captured together are offered for sale, which is a convenient situation for observing their relationship in captivity. Such a pairing offers the nano-reef hobbyist the chance to maintain a truly unique partnership in the animal kingdom.

Feeding snapping and mantis shrimp in captivity is best accomplished with natural, live prey items that they would encounter in the wild. This, of course, is impossible for most hobbyists to accomplish, so the next best thing is to offer small guppies and grass shrimp that have been fed some sort of quality prepared food as a means of increasing their nutritional value. One prey item, up to $1/3$ the length of the predator, fed every other day (more frequently if the prey items are very small in comparison to the predator), will prove adequate.

This particular species of mantis shrimp grows far too large to be housed in a nano-reef over a long period of time. There are, however, colorful species of mantis shrimp originating in the Lower Keys, Caribbean, and Gulf of Mexico that remain small enough to be maintained in a nano-reef for many years.

Chapter Seven

Sessile Invertebrates
for the Nano-Reef Aquarium

Sessile invertebrates are largely what define the reef aquarium. As an experienced marine aquarium hobbyist will attest, corals, clams, tubeworms, and all of the related organisms are the basis of a beautiful reef display.

Many of the sessile invertebrates housed in reef aquaria are hermatypic and so have specific lighting needs. Refer to Part 1 for an explanation of the various aspects of lighting and how it impacts these organisms. When choosing the lighting system for a nano-reef, attention should be paid to the lighting needs of the specific hermatypic invertebrates housed. For instance, mushroom anemones require lower light intensities to survive and thrive than do small-polyped stony corals (SPS). In fact, at the intensities that many SPS corals require, mushroom anemones may actually suffer.

In a large aquarium, the hobbyist can keep organisms with dissimilar light requirements together by placing them at different depths below the bulbs. In the nano-reef, this is generally not a simple task, owing to the relative shallowness of the aquarium. Therefore, it makes sense to keep like animals together, so to speak. If your main interest lies with zoanthids, mushrooms, and other colonial polyps, limit the lighting to one or two power compact lamps that provide actinic and daylight spectra and exclude *Tridacna* and *Hippopus* clams, SPS, and LPS corals from the aquarium.

To keep these light-loving hermatypic invertebrates in a nano-reef, consider multiple power compact lamps and/or a small metal halide fixture for lighting, making sure to provide adequate cooling with surface current and the use of a chiller.

Table 7.1. Overview of Sessile Invertebrate Care in Nano-Reef Aquaria			
Group	Suggested Level of Experience	Lighting Requirements	Remarks
Zoanthids	Beginner	Low to Modest	Can withstand less than ideal water conditions for brief periods of time
Corallimorph-arians		Low to Modest	Can withstand less than ideal water conditions for brief periods of time.
Annelid Worms		None	Require feeding at regular intervals to ensure survival.
Chordates		None	Require feeding at regular intervals to ensure survival.
Octocorals	Intermediate	Modest	Can withstand less than ideal water conditions for brief periods of time.
Actinarians		Modest to Intense	Require feeding at regular intervals to ensure survival.
Scleractinians	Advanced	Intense	Require intense lighting and adherence to optimal water parameters.
Bivalves		None to Intense	Can withstand less than ideal water conditions for brief periods of time.
Poriferans		None	Require feeding at regular intervals to ensure survival.

Invertebrate Selection

Choosing compatible sessile invertebrates is once again of main concern to the nano-reef hobbyist, not only because of the lighting requirements outlined above, but also because placing certain animals within close proximity of each other can lead to tissue damage and the death of a specimen. In addition, the growth rate of some invertebrates may require frequent "pruning" by propagation or else they overgrow hermatypic invertebrates and block their exposure to light. *Xenia*, in particular, are adept at this.

Following is a brief overview of the various types of sessile invertebrates likely to be encountered by marine aquarium hobbyists. Although the information presented will provide a general overview of each phylum, class, or subclass discussed, this information is easily summarized for the nano-reef hobbyist in table form. (See Table 7.1.)

ANTHOZOANS

This is a diverse class with several groups well represented within the ornamental aquarium trade. Both hermatypic and ahermatypic species are found in the class Anthozoa.

ZOANTHIDS

These small animals resemble anemones in that they are small and polyp-like. They may occur singly or in colonies, and they lack a rigid skeleton. The range of colors of zoanthids is spectacular, with some varieties exhibiting different or contrasting colors of the tissue in their tentacles, oral disc, and/or mouth. The polyp size of the various species also differs, though fully grown members of a colony are essentially uniform in size. Interestingly, even different-colored individuals within a colony show general uniformity of size.

Zoanthids come in an assortment of colors. All are fairly easy to keep, and they will reproduce and spread over available space rather quickly.

Zoanthids are comparatively easy to care for, requiring relatively low lighting intensity to survive, and are able to tolerate less than ideal water quality for longer periods of time compared to many other anthozoans. They do not appear to suffer under intense light as corallimorpharians do, though it does not, in my experience, increase the rate at which they grow or reproduce, either. Zoanthids reproduce sexually (by releasing eggs and sperm cells), but asexual budding appears to be far more commonplace and leads to the gradual spreading of the colonies throughout the aquarium. For this reason, the hobbyist on a limited budget may find another reason to consider these creatures for placement in his or her nano-reef. Oftentimes, two or more varieties are seen sitting amongst each other, giving the appearance of a wild flower garden. In all, zoanthids are a great choice of hermatypic sessile invertebrates for novice reef hobbyists; even hobbyists with years of experience rarely tire of their beauty and ease of care.

> ## A Nano-Note on Zooplankton
> Feeding zoanthids a zooplankton food, such as one containing cyclops, may be performed once each week, though adequate lighting and regular partial water changes may obviate the need for supplementary feeding completely.

CORALLIMORPHARIANS

Also lacking a skeleton, corallimorpharians may exist singly or in colonies. They do not bear much resemblance to anemones, but instead have more of a flattened oral disc that ranges from smooth to being

As with zoanthids, mushroom anemones come in a wide assortment of colors. They also exhibit quite a variety of textures as well (i.e., hairy, pimpled, smooth). These are brown smooth mushrooms.

covered in minute tentacles of various shapes and descriptions. The most variety of coloration within the order belongs to the genus *Actinodiscus*, which comprises species of red, green, and blue, and shades thereof. Many have spots or radial stripes of contrasting coloration, adding to their uniqueness. Most members of this genus have oral discs that remain below 3 inches (7.5 cm) in diameter, though some may grow larger in particularly favorable conditions.

Members of the genus *Rhodactis* (sometimes sold under the common name "frilly mushrooms" due to the appearance of their oral discs) tend to grow larger than the aforementioned genus and are noted for their predatory tendencies. Though they house zooxanthellae, it is not uncommon to observe a *Rhodactis* polyp rapidly folding its oral disc over small prey in order to capture it. This is the same method of prey capture utilized by polyps of the genus *Amplexidiscus*, which grow too large to house in even the largest nano-reef aquaria. These should be left for placement in larger, more spacious systems.

Another genus of note is *Ricordia*, whose oral discs are completely covered with tiny, semi-spherical tentacles, giving each polyp the appearance of a miniature carpet anemone.

Pictured are two color forms of Ricordia *mushrooms, red and green.*

Ricordia species exhibit many colors and patterns. Some range from blue to green, while others may be completely orange or have purple tentacles near the mouth, surrounded with a ring of orange tentacles near the margin of the oral disc. Unlike *Actinodiscus* and *Rhodactis* species, which are usually offered as several individuals on a piece of lava rock, *Ricordia* polyps are typically sold as individuals. They are more expensive than most varieties of the former genera, but their appearance justifies their price.

Corallimorpharians, in general, will reproduce under favorable conditions and spread their species throughout the aquarium. *Ricordia* species tend to reproduce with the lowest frequency, while some of the *Rhodactis* species can be quite prolific (to the point of becoming a nuisance if not transplanted to other aquaria). As with zoanthids, an entire nano-reef dedicated to corallimorpharians is quite impressive in appearance. The sheer variety of colors and shapes is enough to capture the attention of hobbyists of all experience levels.

Corallimorpharians kept under adequate light seem to require no additional feeding, though some hobbyists may choose to offer *Rhodactis* species small pieces of fish or shrimp on occasion. Other nano-reef compatible members of this class seem to thrive without feeding at all and apparently obtain all of the necessary nutrients and energy from proper lighting and regular partial water changes.

OCTOCORALS

Members of this subclass are characterized by having small polyps, each with eight arms. Rather than secreting

---

A Nano-Note on Mushrooms

Another trait that corallimorpharians share with zoanthids is their ability to tolerate poor water quality for relatively lengthy periods of time. This makes them a perfect choice for novice reef hobbyists.

Xenia, *an octocoral, is probably the most common and easily recognized member of the group.*

A Nano Note on Noxious Species

We have already seen that certain soft corals secrete toxins into the water for the purpose of eliminating nearby competing coral species. That being the case, keep noxious species only with those corals noted for being tolerant of their toxins. Refer back to our discussion on compatibility for information on this subject.

a hard, calcium carbonate skeleton in the manner that stony corals do, many soft corals create an internal skeleton of calcium spicules to provide form and strength to their tissue. In contrast, gorgonians create a skeleton with the appearance of wood; the material is composed of a fibrous protein called "gorgonin."

Relative to stony corals, most octocorals are hardy and have modest lighting requirements. Many species grow rapidly (in the grand scheme of coral growth rates) under favorable conditions, which can be good or bad in a nano-reef depending on the manner in which it was initially aquascaped or how close corals were placed to one another. They also tend to be less expensive than their stony coral relatives. A nano-reef can be stocked with several small octocorals for a modest price, and it may take only a few months for the reef to mature and fill in with their growth.

One of the most popular varieties of octocorals in the aquarium hobby is undoubtedly *Xenia*, to which you have already been introduced. *Xenia* appear to present a dichotomy to hobbyists: They either thrive and attempt to colonize every available surface in the aquarium, or they die back and disappear. Moderate water current, strong lighting, and regular addition of an iodine supplement seem to greatly increase the chances of the hobbyist's success with *Xenia*, perhaps too much, for they can quickly get out of control in even the largest reef aquaria and begin to overgrow other sessile invertebrates. In captivity, *Xenia* seem to increase their numbers mainly by moving from rock to rock, leaving a small fragment of tissue behind that develops into a complete new colony within the span of a few short weeks. Another method occasionally seen is the twisting-off of a tentacle by water currents, whereupon the tentacle settles on a rock and grows into a complete new colony. This takes several months. Whatever the method of reproduction, the end result requires that new colonies be transplanted to other aquaria in order to avoid a situation in which the *Xenia* come into contact with other anthozoans; scleractinians in particular appear to be harmed by contact with *Xenia* polyps. There is a strong demand in the reef hobby for *Xenia* colonies, however, and a hobbyist who has perfected his or her cultivation of *Xenia* can easily trade with other hobbyists for new coral fragments, cuttings, and polyps.

For the intermediate reef aquarium hobbyist, octocorals may be considered a viable group of introductory corals with which to gain experience on the way to scleractinians. While many species will eventually outgrow their nano-reef homes and need to be moved to more spacious quarters, clippings from the mother colony may be placed back in the nano-reef to continue life there.

Octocorals appreciate occasional feeding with a zooplankton-based food. The same one used for zoanthids will do quite nicely. Their tentacles and polyps will be seen contracting as prey is captured from the passing current, and after a few moments the polyps will re-open to wait for more food particles. Some species will extend a "feeding net" of sorts at night to capture prey; the nets are extended into the water and carried by the prevailing water current, and after a few moments, the nets are retracted back into the coral's crown to remove the food particles. This process can continue for hours and is fascinating to observe.

ACTINARIANS

These true sea anemones are essentially enlarged versions of solitary coral polyps. They all lack a skeleton and may exist singly or as colonies. They may be thought of as complex bags of water, which expand to maximize the exposure of the zooxanthellae in their tissues to light, and occasionally contract completely to expel water and pollutants built up inside their bodies. It might be alarming to see an anemone shrink down into little more than a flat, fleshy mass, but rest assured that in an hour or two the animal will be back to its normal appearance.

While anemones are beautiful and interesting, they can be rather difficult to keep alive in aquariums. Also, remember that anemonefishes, like these false percula clowns (Amphiprion percula), don't need them in aquaria.

The Trouble with *Aiptasia*

Newcomers to the reef aquarium hobby may purchase live rock and be pleased to discover that it already has one or more small anemones growing on it. Ranging in color from cream to root beer, these anemones open during the day and don't wander over the live rock, so the hobbyist is pleased with the surprise. A well-meaning hobbyist usually begins feeding these anemones, believing them to be desirable, but this is unfortunately not the case at all. These anemones belong to the genus *Aiptasia*, sometimes called rock or glass anemones but usually referred to by

their genus name. *Aiptasia* seem harmless enough until they start stinging sessile invertebrates or conditions become suitable for their reproduction. In the case of the former, the stinging tentacles of an Aiptasia (regardless of how large or small) will irritate or damage the tissue of nearby anthozoans, causing their polyps to remain retracted and therefore exposed to less light and food; by the same token, hermatypic clams that are stung by these anemones do not fully extend their mantle tissue. When *Aiptasia* begin reproducing, the problem quickly escalates and gets out of hand. In the confines of a nano-reef in which hobbyists are likely to squeeze as much invertebrate life as possible, there simply is no place for *Aiptasia*. There are a few remedies to the problem. First, choose live rock that appears to be completely free of these anemones, as even the smallest specimens can eventually grow much larger and become more problematic. If you notice these anemones at any point, consider the use of a biological controller to eat them, such as the peppermint shrimp (*Lysmata wurdemanni*), which happily eats small *Aiptasia* and is easily fed as per other ornamental shrimp when the anemones appear to be gone. These shrimp leave other anthozoans alone and are considered reef-safe. Chemical means of killing *Aiptasia* include squirting supersaturated kalkwasser solution onto the oral disc and tentacles of the anemone, causing the anemone to contract and hence ingest the kalkwasser, killing it. While this tactic has relatively little impact on water chemistry in large aquaria, employing it in a nano-reef is likely to cause a rapid increase in pH which can easily cause distress or even death to desirable livestock, and is therefore not recommended. Another chemical method is a product sold specifically to kill these anemones, having no obvious impact on the water quality or to desirable anthozoans in the vicinity of the *Aiptasia*; see your local aquarium store for details.

Of the anemone species available to hobbyists, only a few are compatible with nano-reef aquaria. The remaining species grow far too large for placement in such small systems. The common Caribbean anemones of the genus *Condylactis* remain relatively small and have modest lighting requirements, making them the best choice for placement in nano-reef aquaria. This is one anemone that is recommended for placement in a nano-reef. They are hardy (relative to other anemone species), colorful, inexpensive, and readily available.

The only other member of this class that should be considered as remotely compatible with nano-reef aquaria is the bubble-tip anemone (*Entacmaea quadricolor*). They are by no means as hardy as some of the aforementioned groups of anthozoans discussed in this chapter. However, they are generally able to withstand conditions likely to present themselves in a

Scleractinians need strong lighting and good water quality in order to thrive in any reef system—especially a nano-reef system.

nano-reef and thrive with intense light and adequate water quality. Of course, don't forget the discussion earlier about the tendency of these anemones to wander.

The feeding of anemones should be performed once each week with a small piece of fresh fish or shrimp. Do not offer cooked flesh, which is often eaten and then "spit out" within a few minutes. Fortifying the flesh by soaking it in a vitamin solution or stuffing it with quality fish food flakes or nori (seaweed) is a worthwhile procedure that helps ensure the long-term survival of the anemone in your aquarium, regardless of total volume.

SCLERACTINIANS

This group constitutes the stony corals, both large-polyped and small-polyped, LPS and SPS, respectively. Stony corals are so called because they secrete a skeletal structure of aragonite (similar to calcite or lime stone) beneath their tissue. Stony corals are largely responsible for building reefs and are probably one of the first types of invertebrates that come to mind when the average person thinks of a reef environment.

In captivity, scleractinians require that a few conditions be met in order to survive and grow. They must have proper lighting; adequate water circulation; water temperature not exceeding 84°F (28.5°C) for extended periods of time; adequate alkalinity to maintain stable pH; natural seawater concentrations of major, minor, and trace elements; and enough space between them and a neighboring coral that the two colonies are not in physical contact at any time. In short, they must be maintained within a true replicated reef setting, and although this seems fundamental, it is not always easy to achieve within the confines of a nano-reef. Once again, limited water volume plays a role in maintaining delicate reef creatures, and stony corals reside at or near the top of this list. The nano-reef templates presented in the next chapter outline just such a system.

Large-polyped stony (LPS) corals tend to be a bit more difficult to maintain in nano-reefs compared to the many SPS coral species. This is largely a result of the fact that large-polyped species sweep an area around themselves at night with specialized tentacles to kill encroaching corals. Such a tactic requires that these defensive species be given plenty of room around their perimeter free of other corals, and thus places further limitations on the hobbyist's attempts to stock his or her nano-reef. LPS corals of the genera *Galaxea* and *Lobophyllia* are good examples of such aggressive species. In addition, many large-polyped corals contract at night and expand during the day to nearly twice their contracted size; they, too, must be kept away from nearby corals to avoid damaging them. Of particular note in this category are corals in the genera *Cataphyllia* and *Trachyphyllia*. If your intention is to maintain

This purple-tipped Acropora *coral colony is the result of good-quality water and plenty of light. Of course, it helps to get a healthy specimen from the start, too.*

LPS corals in a nano-reef, look for small specimens and be sure to give them plenty of room. They are beautiful organisms to the last and certainly warrant consideration for nano-reef placement.

Small-polyped stony (SPS) corals should also be given ample room, but generally not as much as is required for their LPS counterparts. The counterintuitive aspect of SPS husbandry is that some species grow so rapidly under favorable conditions that it may be necessary to move them within the span of a few weeks or months. If you have corals growing at such a rate, they are apparently enjoying the conditions in that precise location, and moving them should be avoided. There are times when you will have no choice but to relocate corals in order to prevent them from being crowded, and when this occurs, it is sensible to place the coral in a location with similar lightir flow characteristics to that from which it was m

...eed ample room to grow,
...ot as much as the various
...corals require.

One of the best means of starting a true SPS themed nano-reef is to purchase coral frags from experienced hobbyists. Not only does this decrea need to collect corals from a natural reef, but it enables the hobbyist to stock a wide variety of sp minimal cost. Corals of the genera *Acropora*, *Mor Stylophora*, *Porites*, *Seriatopora*, and *Hydnophora* e many different colors and growth forms (from pla appearance of a bottle-cleaning brush) and are rea available from frag-swapping organizations as well as many

These worms utilize their gills, which have a feathery appearance, to filter water-borne particles from the passing currents.

cutting-edge retailers. Of the six genera mentioned above, *Acropora* and *Montipora* are generally considered to be the fastest growing and most durable.

In general, it can be said that SPS corals are easier to maintain in captivity than most LPS species. I believe this is largely related to the health of the coral upon delivery. LPS corals often suffer damage in the bag during transit[1], and this can lead to tissue degeneration and ultimately death of the entire colony. For this reason, *all* prospective coral purchases should be inspected carefully for tissue damage, and if any is present, it should provide reason for pause on the transaction. Damaged tissue can sometimes regenerate in favorable conditions, but in the nano-reef setting, the odds will be stacked against you and the coral. Leave such a coral where it is for someone with a larger aquarium to consider.

Feed LPS corals as you would an anemone, and SPS corals as for zoanthids. Doing so will increase the diversity of nutrients available to the corals and can be a crucial factor behind their long-term survival in an aquarium with limited lighting means. Remember that overfeeding leads to deteriorating water quality, which is more harmful to the corals than not feeding them at all. Don't overfeed!

ANNELID WORMS

These animals are sometimes referred to as segmented worms. They are separated into two subclasses—those that are motile (subclass Errantia) and those that are sedentary (subclass Sedentaria). The focus of this section is on the sedentary annelids, represented in marine aquaria principally by Christmas tree worms (*Spirobranchus* sp.), tubeworms (*Pomatostegus* sp., *Hydroides* sp., *Protula* sp.), and feather dusters (*Sabellastarte* sp., *Bispira* sp.). Other sedentary annelid worms that are commonly seen in reef aquaria are terebellid worms (sometimes referred to as spaghetti worms in literature) and their allies. Terebellid worms utilize sticky tentacles to search crevices in live rock and live sand for particles of food, and the tentacles are then retracted to the worm's mouth for feeding. Terebellid worms are incidental introductions to reef aquaria via live rock and are not offered for sale individually. However, this is certainly not the case with feather dusters and their allies.

Filter-feeding sedentary worms are quite simple to care for. They generally require feeding several times each week with a phytoplankton or zooplankton suspension to remain healthy. However, the needs of an individual are relatively modest. Obviously, the larger the worm is, the more food it will require; additionally, aquaria with numerous filter-feeding worms must receive a considerable amount of food. In a nano-reef, it is best to house only one large variety of filter-feeding worms, such as a Hawaiian feather duster (*Sabellastarte* sp.) or a small colony of two to four Christmas tree worms, to minimize the chances of exceeding the rate of nutrient removal by the biological and chemical filtration.

Feather dusters are filter-feeding sedentary worms that are commonly available to hobbyists.

In terms of hardiness relative to other sessile ornamental marine invertebrates, filter-feeding worms are somewhere in the middle of the group. They are very quick to retract their plume of gills into their tube at the slightest shadow overhead, which helps them avoid predation from angelfishes and other families that like to eat these worms' gill filaments. A stressed worm may discard the plume, grow a new one, and resume life as usual, or not open to feed for days and eventually perish. If the worm has perished, you will often see it hanging limp from its tube. If you don't notice this, leave the tube alone; chances are that in a few weeks a new plume will emerge from the tube, which will get larger with time. Minimize stress to these worms by not keeping them in the same nano-reef aquaria as angelfishes and ornamental crabs (not hermit crabs, which generally leave these worms alone). Additionally, some species of ornamental shrimp have been known to eat the occasional gill filament of a filter-feeding worm, so exercise caution when pairing them in

Livestock

157

PART TWO

the same aquarium, and be prepared to move the worm or the shrimp if you observe them bothering it.

In addition to regular feeding, those filter-feeding worms secreting a calcareous tube require natural seawater concentrations of calcium and adequate alkalinity. Regular partial water changes are recommended to maintain these concentrations and decrease the amount of latent organic material in the water. These worms are somewhat sensitive to poor water quality, so every effort should be made to keep the concentrations of waste materials as low as possible.

ASCIDIACEANS

Belonging to the phylum Chordata, ascidiaceans are comprised of tunicates, or sea squirts. Tunicates are essentially bell-shaped animals that may exist as individuals or in colonies. They have a pair of siphons through which water enters and exits the animal, bringing in food and dissolved oxygen. The range of sizes and colors in which tunicates are known to exist is quite impressive. Some are the size of a pea, while others may be kiwi fruit-sized or larger, and colors can range from translucent with bright-colored margins to opaque and dull. In all cases, tunicates exist attached to some substrate such as a rock or piling. They require moderate care, mostly as a result of the need for a planktonic diet and good water conditions. In this regard they are similar to the filter-feeding worms discussed in the previous section. In fact, all remarks related to the feeding and care of those worms apply to the tunicates, also.

Some ascidians are almost transparent, which can be easily seen by looking at this beautiful specimen.

BIVALVES

Technically referred to as bivalves, clams, scallops, mussels, oysters, and some other lesser known animals are familiar to nearly everyone. Within the reef aquarium setting in general, this book is principally interested in the giant clams of the family Tridacnidae and the scallops of the genus *Lima*.

The giant clams are hermatypic, housing zooxanthellae in their mantle tissues. In addition, cells in the mantle contain UV-protective pigments that give these clams their dazzling array of colors and patterns. A healthy clam in the proper location will open and expose its mantle to aquarium lighting so that zooxanthellae can undergo photosynthesis and produce food. A clam that appears to be straining to open as widely as possible may be underexposed to light and trying to increase its exposure; in this case, increase lighting intensity gradually by moving the clam closer to the light source and observe its reaction over a period of at least one week. If during

Tridacnid clams, such as the Tridacna crocea *shown, are on most reef aquarium hobbyists' list of desirable sessile invertebrates to keep, but they are generally more demanding of water quality, feeding, and light intensity than the majority of nano-reef hobbyists can manage over the long term. Small specimens may be maintained in nano-reefs for a period of time, but they generally require removal to a larger system if expected to survive for several years.*

Clams that are wide open all the time or seem to be straining to open their mantles as far as possible may be underexposed to light and should be moved to a more light-intense area of the aquarium.

that time the clam still appears to be opening as widely as possible, it might be an indication that additional light bulbs are needed to increase the intensity of light in the aquarium.

If the converse situation occurs (i.e., the clam appears to keep mostly closed while the lights are on), the clam may be attempting to shield the zooxanthellae from too much light. When zooxanthellae are exposed to light and begin to photosynthesize, they produce oxygen. Excessive oxygen production may irritate the clam's mantle tissue, so it appears to try and avoid this occurrence by only exposing a portion of the mantle to the light. In this instance, it is suggested that you move the clam further from the light source, and if this is not possible, it will be necessary to decrease lighting intensity in the nano-reef by replacing one of the bulbs with a lower-intensity bulb.

The mantle of the Tridacnid clams features both a prominent inhalant and exhalent siphon, through which water rich in oxygen and dissolved nutrients and containing suspended particles is actively pumped. Tridacnid clams are believed to be able to remove dissolved nutrients directly from the water, and many hobbyists have attempted to utilize this ability to their benefit by employing a large number of

A Nano-Note on Scallops

In general, scallops seem to exhibit the same sort of dichotomy discussed earlier with reference to *Xenia*—they either thrive for years or perish within a few days or weeks of being placed in an aquarium.

clams in a reef aquarium to help with nutrient management. In theory, an aspiring hobbyist could use this facet of Tridacnid clams to their advantage in large nano-reef aquaria with intense illumination.

There are six species of Tridacnid clams commonly available to hobbyists, though others exist. They are: *Tridacna crocea, T. derasa, T. gigas, T. maxima, T. squamosa,* and *Hippopus hippopus.* Of these, *T. derasa* and *H. hippopus* tend to be the easiest to maintain and are therefore considered good choices for the sometimes volatile environment encountered in a nano-reef. The keys to long-term success with Tridacnid clams are identical to those for scleractinians.

Flame scallops (*Lima* sp.) are not hermatypic, and they rely on particles passing in the currents for sustenance. They, like most other bivalves, are filter feeders, and they may be fed in the same fashion as tunicates. The factors that help determine the fate of a scallop are largely the health of the animal at the time that it is placed into the aquarium and whether or not it receives adequate feeding once there. Avoid scallops (and other bivalves, for that matter) with any sort of obvious damage to the mantle tissue; purchasing such an animal is asking for disappointment, for these damaged specimens rarely survive for more than a few days or weeks in an aquarium. Otherwise, a healthy scallop should remain so for one or more years and requires only that the water quality be up to par with the needs of octocorals. Scallops are interesting and colorful bivalves that do well in the nano-reef aquarium.

Giant clams are also filter feeders, though they seem to rely on this method of nutrient uptake as a secondary course. So long as the lighting intensity in the nano-reef appears to suit their needs, feeding giant clams once every other week with a planktonic suspension will typically prove adequate to maintain long-term health.

Similar to feather dusters, flame scallops rely on suspended particles in the aquarium's water to feed them. While we consider flame scallops to be sessile, they can move themselves for short distances if disturbed.

PORIFERANS

More commonly known as sponges, poriferans are the most basic multicellular life forms on the planet, essentially consisting of individual cells acting in unison to create a weak current that carries water and food particles into the sponge itself. The material that is the structure of the overall sponge is either one or a combination of hard spicules or resilient protein (spongin). The spicules of some encrusting species appear to be largely composed of silicate, and many a hobbyist has reached under a piece of fresh live rock and been impaled with these glass-like shards. Your best bet is to beware and use tough gloves or heavy towels when handling uncured live rock or that which has been residing inside a reef aquarium for several months.

Sponges can grow in many forms. This bowl-shaped sponge is a deepwater species that is better left in the ocean.

The majority of sponges offered for sale in the aquarium originate in relatively shallow water and are bright yellow, orange, red, pink, purple, or blue in coloration. Depending on the physical conditions in the environment from which they were collected, sponges may grow in encrusting forms or as free-standing structures, as well as some other forms. While there are many species of sponge available for purchase as individuals, a far greater diversity of species can be had by purchasing quality uncured live rock, particularly that from the Atlantic and Caribbean, and using it to seed a new aquarium once it has been properly cured. Such rock is often colonized with an impressive array of sponges and other encrusting invertebrates that are able to survive shipping well enough to recover in favorable conditions.

Once again, the dichotomy rears its ugly head with sponges, for they either do well in captivity and grow at a steady rate or gradually perish to leave nothing behind but spongin and spicules. The key to keeping sponges alive is adequate food in the water. In order to maintain them in a nano-reef, the system should be fed daily with a planktonic suspension and employ aggressive protein skimming and biological filtration to maintain immeasurable concentrations of dissolved organic materials. Additionally, sponges benefit from the presence of silicate in the water, and though you might be inclined to think that silicate-rich water will encourage the growth of diatoms, this tends not to be the case in aquaria housing an ample population of ornamental sponges or those that are introduced incidentally on live rock.

Sponges exposed to air inevitably trap air in their pores, which leads to death of the surrounding tissue. For this reason, never expose sponges to air.

Chapter Eight

Creating A Balanced

Nano-Reef Ecosystem

By now, it should be apparent that quite a few decisions must be made to create an aquarium ecosystem in which the inhabitants are compatible and compliment each other's presence. To do this, you must avoid the temptation to take a trip down to the local aquarium shop on the day that its marine livestock shipment arrives and make selections based solely on the appearance of a fish or invertebrate. Such an approach will inevitably lead to the loss of marine life and your money. Taking what has been covered in the preceding two parts of this book, you should be able to make informed decisions about compatible species selection for your new nano-reef.

Let's take it one step further, however, and present a method that is commonly used when planning a new aquarium, regardless of the overall volume of the system. It may seem a bit excessive to take such pains when planning this sort of setup, but this attention to detail is one of the things that has enabled so many hobbyists to enjoy success as a marine aquarium hobbyist.

Steps for Setting Up a New Aquarium

The basic steps of setting up a new aquarium are as follows:

STEP 1—DETERMINE WHERE THE AQUARIUM WILL BE SITUATED

The aquarium should be placed in an area where people can sit and enjoy it, but not where there will be excessive foot traffic. Consider the support equipment needed and where it will be housed. For instance, lighting ballasts or a chiller unit should be concealed to avoid detracting from the appearance of the aquarium itself. A stand with cabinet space to house these items is therefore recommended. Make sure that one or more electrical outlets are nearby and that the circuits can carry the load that will be placed on them when all equipment is in operation. Because sunlight directly hitting an aquarium can rapidly cause the water temperature to rise (particularly in small systems), it is recommended that the nano-reef be placed in a location in which sunlight will not strike it. By the same token, small aquaria placed directly in front of a house's outside wall that receives several hours of direct sunlight daily sometimes overheat as a result of the irradiance of heat from the wall itself.

Step 1—Aquarium placement.

STEP 2—ENSURE ADEQUATE SPACE

Ensure that adequate space exists behind the aquarium and cabinet to allow hang-on-the-back filters, electrical cords, and/or flexible tubing to be placed.

STEP 3—MIX THE SEA WATER

Mix up enough sea water using purified water and a high-quality synthetic salt blend to fill the entire volume of the nano-reef and any external filters and chillers employed. This water should be allowed to mix for several hours to allow dissolved gasses formed during dissolution of the salt to escape into the atmosphere. Adjust the specific gravity of the seawater to approximately 1.021 g/cm^3, and ensure that the pH and alkalinity of the water are within the required ranges. A heater placed in the mixing vessel and set to approximately 77°F (26°C) will adjust the water to the proper temperature for adding live rock and live sand.

STEP 4—RINSE THE AQUARIUM

Rinse out the inside of the aquarium with tap water, and turn it over to allow most of the water to drip out.

STEP 5—AQUARIUM PLACEMENT ON THE STAND

Now that the new aquarium is completely rinsed out, you can go ahead and place the aquarium on the cabinet. Be sure to check to make sure that it is level, as well.

STEP 6—FILL THE AQUARIUM

Once your aquarium is placed on its stand and you have checked to make sure that it is level all the way around, you can fill it about halfway with the pre-mixed sea water.

STEP 7—EQUIPMENT PLACEMENT

Place all non-lighting equipment in the desired locations within the aquarium. This includes the protein skimmer,

Step 6—Fill the aquarium.

heater, submersible pumps or powerheads, intake and exhaust tubes from the chiller, and so on.

STEP 8—UTILIZE LIVE SAND OR ARAGONITE BASE

If live sand or regular aragonite sand is being used, add it to the aquarium now. Allow a few minutes for any dust in the sand to settle out of suspension, which would otherwise obscure your view of live rock placement.

STEP 9—LIVE ROCK PLACEMENT

Place live rock in the aquarium in the desired arrangement. Keep in mind the requirements of whatever livestock you have chosen to keep for shelter or placement, and arrange the rock accordingly.

STEP 10—PRIME THE EQUIPMENT

Add sea water to the appropriate support equipment (i.e. protein skimmer reaction column, refugium, filters, chiller, etc.).

Step 9—Place live rock.

STEP 11—TOP OFF AQUARIUM

Fill the aquarium the rest of the way with the sea water. To help prevent accidental water spillage when working in the aquarium, the depth of water should be no closer than 1 inch (2.5 cm) to the very top of the aquarium.

STEP 12—LIGHTING PLACEMENT AND FINAL CHECK

Place canopy and/or lighting over the nano-reef, set timers to control the light cycle, and then plug them in. Stand back for a brief moment and check to make sure that nothing is immediately wrong (i.e., the tank is not leaking, all of the equipment is there, the lighting has ignited, etc.). Now plug in all electrical support equipment and ensure that it is operating as intended. You should sit back and watch the tank for at least 15 or 20 minutes to ensure that the aquarium's equipment is not sprouting any leaks or the hose did not become dislodged, etc.

STEP 13—CHEMICAL CHECKS

Wait a few days to ensure that the concentrations of ammonia and nitrite are immeasurable before adding any ornamental livestock whatsoever. Once you are satisfied that these conditions have been met, you may begin gradually adding ornamental livestock to the nano-reef.

Final chemical checks.

That's all there is to it! It might sound complicated at first, but it is really nothing more than common sense and sound principles of aquarium husbandry. Following these steps will provide the basis of a successful nano-reef every time.

Five Templates of Systems Outlined

The following pages show some examples of standard templates employed by professionals who give advice to novice hobbyists or those venturing into nano-reef setups for the first time. By using these as examples and then making your own templates in a similar fashion, you will have taken the first step toward creating a stable and tranquil nano-reef. The second step in this process is adhering to what you have decided. If you have larger aquaria within which to move some organism out of the nano-reef, thereby making room for a prospective new purchase, then by all means make the purchase, as long as the newcomer is compatible with remaining livestock in the nano-reef.

TEMPLATE I: 2.5-GALLON (9.45 L) ZOANTHID REEF AQUARIUM

2.5-gallon (9.45 l) acrylic aquarium.

FILTRATION
Chemical Filtration — Hang-on-the-back fluidized-bed media filter loaded with a resin that absorbs organic material.
Biological Filtration — Live rock and live sand (see below).

LIGHTING
2 x 9-watt Power Compact Lamps
1 x 9-watt actinic lamp set on a timer to operate from 9 a.m. to 7 p.m., 1 x 9-watt daylight lamp set on a timer to operate from 10 a.m. to 6 p.m., and 1 clip-on LED moonlight lamp set on a timer to operate from 10 p.m. to 6 a.m.

HEATING
1 x 25-watt submersible heater.

WATER CIRCULATION
From the direct exhaust of the fluidized-bed filter across aquarium surface.

INFRASTRUCTURE
Live Rock
3–5 lbs (1.35-2.5 kg) of cured, low-density live rock.
Live Sand or Aragonite Sand (which becomes live with time)
Enough to completely cover the bottom $^{1}/_{2}$" (2.5 cm) of the aquarium.

LIVESTOCK
Sessile Invertebrates
Several colonies of different-colored zoanthids placed with at least 1" (5 cm) of space surrounding perimeters of each colony to enable the colonies to spread with time.
Motile Invertebrates
2 x Scarlet Cleaner Shrimp (*Lysmata amboinensis*) or Peppermint Shrimp (*L. wurdemanni*).
Grazers, Scavengers, and Sand-Sifters
3 x Paper Bubble Shells (*Bulla* sp.).
1 x Scarlet Reef Hermit Crab (*Paguristes cadenati*).

TEMPLATE II: 3-GALLON (11.34 L) MIXED ZOANTHID AND CORALLIMORPHARIAN NANO-REEF AQUARIUM

3-gallon (11.34 l) acrylic aquarium.

FILTRATION
Chemical Filtration — Hang-on-the-back fluidized-bed media filter loaded with a resin that absorbs organic material.
Biological Filtration — Live rock and live sand.

LIGHTING
1 x 18-watt dual actinic/daylight power compact lamp that is set on a timer to operate from 9 a.m. to 7 p.m. and clip-on LED moonlight lamp that is set on a timer to operate from 10 p.m. to 6 a.m.

HEATING
1 x 25-watt submersible heater.

WATER CIRCULATION
Water movement from internal return pump located in overflow.

INFRASTRUCTURE
Live Rock
4–7 lbs (1.8-3.15 kg) of cured, low-density live rock.
Live Sand or Aragonite Sand
Enough to completely cover the bottom $^1/_2$" (2.5 cm) of the aquarium.

LIVESTOCK
Sessile Invertebrates
Several colonies of different-colored zoanthids and corallimorpharians, placed with at least 1" (5 cm) of space surrounding perimeters of each colony to enable the colonies to spread with time.
Motile Invertebrates
2 x Fire Shrimp (*Lysmata debelius*).
Grazers, Scavengers, and Sand-Sifters
3 x Paper Bubble Shells (*Bulla* sp.).
1 x Scarlet Reef Hermit Crab (*Paguristes cadenati*).

TEMPLATE III: 7.5-GALLON (28.35 L) MIXED NANO-REEF AQUARIUM

7.5-gallon (28.35 l) glass aquarium.

FILTRATION
Chemical Filtration — Hang-on-the-back protein skimmer.
Biological Filtration — Live rock, live sand, and a refugium.

LIGHTING
1 x 18-watt actinic power compact lamp that is set on a timer to operate from 9 a.m. to 7 p.m., 1 x 18-watt daylight power compact lamp that is set on a timer to operate from 10 a.m. to 6 p.m., and a built-in LED moonlight lamp, which is set on a timer to operate from 10 p.m. to 6 a.m.

HEATING
1 x 25-watt submersible heater.

WATER CIRCULATION
Direct exhaust from protein skimmer and refugium across surface of aquarium.

INFRASTRUCTURE
Live Rock — 9–15 lbs of cured, low-density live rock.
Live Sand or Aragonite Sand — Enough to completely cover the bottom $^1/_2$" (2.5 cm) of the aquarium.

LIVESTOCK
Sessile Invertebrates

1 x small *Sarcophyton* sp. soft coral.	1 x small *Nepthea* sp. soft coral.
1 x small *Sinularia* sp. soft coral.	4 x colonies of assorted zoanthids.
2 x colonies of assorted corallimorpharians.	1 x colony of *Xenia* sp.
1 x colony of *Rhodactis* sp.	1 x Hawaiian Feather Duster (*Sabellastarte* sp.).

Fishes

1 x Sixline Wrasse (*Pseudocheilinus hexataenia*).	2 x False Percula Anemonefish (*Amphiprion percula*).

Grazers, Scavengers, and Sand-Sifters

5 x Paper Bubble Shells (*Bulla* sp.).	2 x Scarlet Reef Hermit Crab (*Paguristes cadenati*).

TEMPLATE IV: 10-GALLON (37.58 L) MIXED NANO-REEF AQUARIUM

10-gallon (37.58 l) glass aquarium.

FILTRATION

Chemical Filtration — Hang-on-the-back protein skimmer.
Biological Filtration — Live rock, live sand, and a refugium.

LIGHTING

1 x 18-watt actinic power compact lamp that is set on a timer to operate from 9 a.m. to 7 p.m., 1 x 18-watt daylight power compact lamp that is set on a timer to operate from 10 a.m. to 6 p.m., and a built-in LED moonlight lamp, which is set on a timer to operate from 10 p.m. to 6 a.m.

HEATING

1 x 25-watt submersible heater.

WATER CIRCULATION

Direct exhaust from the protein skimmer and refugium across surface of aquarium.

INFRASTRUCTURE

Live Rock — 12–18 lbs of cured, low-density live rock.
Live Sand or Aragonite Sand — Enough to completely cover the bottom $^1/_2$" (2.5 cm) of the aquarium.

LIVESTOCK

Sessile Invertebrates

1 x small *Nepthea* sp. soft coral.	1 x small *Cladiella* sp. soft coral.
5 x colonies of assorted zoanthids.	3 x colonies of assorted corallimorpharians.
1 x colony of *Xenia* sp.	1 x *Condylactis* sp. anemone.
1 x colony of tunicates.	1 x assorted scallop (*Lima* sp.).

Motile Invertebrates
2 x Peppermint Shrimp (*Lysmata wurdemanni*).

Fishes

1 x Blackcap Gramma (*Gramma melacara*).	1 x Rainford's Goby (*Amblygobius rainfordi*).
1 x Brazilian Flameback Angelfish (*Centropyge aurantonotus*).	

Grazers, Scavengers, Sand-Sifters

5 x Paper Bubble Shells (*Bulla* sp.).	2 x Scarlet Reef Hermit Crab (*Paguristes cadenati*).

Nano-Reef Setup

173

PART THREE

TEMPLATE V: 15-GALLON (56.7 L) TECHNO-REEF AQUARIUM

15-gallon (56.7 l) glass aquarium.

FILTRATION

Chemical Filtration — Hang-on-the-back protein skimmer.

Biological Filtration — Live rock and live sand (see below) and a refugium.

LIGHTING

1 x 150-watt metal halide fixture that is set on a timer to operate from 11 a.m. to 5 p.m., 1 x 18-watt actinic power compact lamp that is set on a timer to operate from 9 a.m. to 7 p.m., 1 x 18-watt daylight power compact lamp that is set on a timer to operate from 10 a.m. to 6 p.m., and a clip-on LED moonlight lamp, which is set on a timer to operate from 10 p.m. to 6 a.m.

HEATING

1 x 25-watt submersible heater.

COOLING

1 x 1/10th-HP chiller.

WATER CIRCULATION

Direct exhaust from protein skimmer and refugium across surface of aquarium.

pH CONTROL

Kalkwasser Reactor.
Electronic pH-Controller.

INFRASTRUCTURE

Live Rock — 18–25 lbs (8.1-11.25 kg) of cured, low-density live rock.

Live Sand or Aragonite Sand — Enough to completely cover the bottom $^1/_2$" (2.5 cm) of the aquarium.

LIVESTOCK

Sessile Invertebrates
3 x *Acropora* sp. stony coral frags.
3 x *Montipora* sp. stony coral frags.
2 x *Porites* sp. stony coral frags.
1 x *Cataphyllia* sp. stony coral.
1 x *Trachyphyllia* sp. stony coral.
1 x *Heliopora* sp. soft coral.
1 x *Tridacna derasa*.
1 x *Hippopus hippopus*.
1 x colony Christmas Tree Worms (*Spirobranchus* sp.).
Motile Invertebrates
2 x Peppermint Shrimp (*Lysmata wurdemanni*)
Fishes
1 x Candy Basslet (*Liopropoma carmabi*).
1 x Solar Fairy Wrasse (*Cirrhilabrus solorensis*).
1 x pair of Banggai Cardinalfish (*Pterapogon. kauderni*).
Grazers, Scavengers, Sand-Sifters
10 x Paper Bubble Shells (*Bulla* sp.).
5 x Scarlet Reef Hermit Crab.

Epilogue

As I sit at my desk and reflect over the information I have presented in this book, I realize that setting up a nano-reef and caring for it may seem an overwhelming task to some. In reality, it's not difficult at all, provided you follow some basic rules:

- Perform regular water changes with seawater prepared from purified water and a quality synthetic salt blend.
- Maintain concentrations of non-conservative ions within the recommended ranges.
- Utilize protein skimming or some other means of organic-material removal from the water.
- Provide adequate lighting intensity, duration, and spectral characteristics to the light-dependent organisms you wish to keep.
- Make wise decisions about livestock to be housed in your nano-reef.
- Do not overstock, overcrowd, or overfeed the aquarium.

That's really all there is to it. This book was written to provide the information needed to make intelligent choices about all aspects of nano-reef care, and hopefully it also increased your understanding of marine aquarium husbandry in general. In that regard, I hope that this book becomes a regular guide to which you refer when a problem or question presents itself. I have enjoyed writing *The Nano-Reef Handbook* and thank you for taking the time to read it. I wish you the best of luck with your nano-reef and all other aquarium-related endeavors!

C.R. Brightwell
Marine Scientist
July, 2005

175

EPILOGUE

Footnotes

CHAPTER 1

[1] At high concentrations, ammonium can burn sensitive tissue. However, this is essentially of concern only in low-pH environments. By the time the ammonium concentration reaches the dangerous level in a pH of seawater, the unionized ammonia will have already killed the livestock.

[2] I have spoken to numerous hobbyists and aquarium professionals maintaining aquaria with nitrate concentrations of several-hundred ppm, in which marine fishes were living seemingly normal lives. It is important to note that the nitrate concentration increased gradually, not all at once, and that sudden decreases in the concentration often killed fish in these systems. Additionally, no fish could be added to the system, as the elevated nitrate concentration would quickly kill them.

CHAPTER 2

[1] This temperature is given for sunlight over the equator at noon. This is relevant because most coral reefs are located within the tropics, hence they receive light of this nature at the water's surface.

[2] Water temperature and gas solubility are inversely related: The higher the temperature of water, the less dissolved gas can exist in it.

CHAPTER 4

[1] Corals, zoanthids, corallimorpharians, anemones, and a few other families that are of little importance to aquarium hobbyists make up the phylum Cnidaria; collectively, these organisms are referred to as cnidarians.

CHAPTER 5

[1] Certain elongate species of fish may be relatively diminutive in overall stature yet measure greater than 3 inches (7.5 cm) total length; as long as they are considered reef-safe, they may be housed in nano-reef aquaria.

[2] Some species have a tendency to eat or harass small hermit crabs and shrimp, decorative filter-feeding worms (such as Christmas tree and fan worms), sea stars, and the mantles of small Tridacnid clams.

[3] The wrasse basslet *(L. eukrines)* and rainbow basslet *(L. fasciatum)* grow too large to be housed in nano-reef aquaria.

[4] A few species are sexually dimorphic, meaning that mature males and females can be easily distinguished from one another on the basis of appearance. Although some hobbyists are able to infer the sex of the Banggai cardinalfish, it is often hit–or–miss, and most species commonly encountered for sale in the U.S. aquarium trade must be kept in a group to allow natural pairing to occur.

[5] Clark's clownfish *(Amphiprion clarkii)* is an exception; adult males and females may be the same size.

[6] Some species are so cryptic that you might swear there are no "'horses" in the aquarium, until the movement of an eye or fin betrays their presence.

CHAPTER 6

[1] A few species of mantis shrimp within the genus *Gonodactylus* prey upon bivalves, which they accomplish by bashing the shell into bits and then eating the tissue. These species feature swollen claws (akin to clubs) rather than spines.

CHAPTER 7

[1] Though small-polyped species can also suffer damage during shipping, they can usually be "treated" by covering broken or bare areas of the skeleton with cyanoacrylate to prevent the development of harmful microbes to the surrounding tissue. Simply spread a thin layer of cyanoacrylate gel to the freshly damaged area with a toothpick, rinse the coral in a tub of seawater from its shipping bag, and place the colony into the aquarium. New coral tissue will cover the cyanoacrylate within a few weeks.

Glossary

Ahermatypic – Describing a type of coral that does not contribute substantially to reef building.

Alkalinity – Having or maintaining a pH higher than 7.

Anemonefishes – Fishes within the subfamily Amphiprionidae

Angelfishes – Fishes within the family Pomacanthidae.

Aragonite – A substance made entirely from calcium carbonate that is secreted by reef-building organisms.

Bio-intermediate – Referring to elements that are constantly replenished by new sea water moving in from other areas of the globe.

Biolimiting – Referring to elements that are rapidly depleted by biological activity.

Biological filtration – A type of water purification that is performed by living organisms, usually bacteria, plants, and cyanobacteria.

Biounlimiting – Referring to elements that are not utilized by living organisms. Also see conservatively.

Blennies – Fishes within the family Blenniidae.

Buffers – Substances responsible for maintaining pH stability.

Calcium – A major inorganic element with an average concentration of approximately 412 parts per million (ppm) in sea water. Calcium is one of the most important elements for reef organisms kept in aquaria.

Calcium carbonate – A salt that has a relatively low solubility in water. Two common forms are calcite and aragonite.

Calcium chloride – A salt that readily dissociates into calcium and chloride atoms.

Cardinalfishes – Fishes within the genus Apogonidae.

Cation – An ion with a positive charge.

Chelated calcium – Calcium molecules bound to a large organic molecule. Examples include calcium-EDTA (ethylenediaminetetraacetic acid) and calcium gluconate.

Conservatively– Refers to elements that are not utilized by living organisms.

Corallimorpharians – Mushroom anemones and their allies.

Cyanobacteria – Blue-green algae. Commonly referred to as "slime algae" in aquariums due to its greasy or slimy appearance.

Damselfishes – Fishes within the family Pomacentridae.

Dartfishes – Fishes within the family Microdesmidae.

Density – The mass of a substance per unit volume. Measured in units of dissolved substances per ml of seawater as specific gravity. A hydrometer is the tool that is used to measure specific gravity.

Dragonets – Fishes within the family Callionymidae.

Dwarf seabasses – Fishes within the family Serranidae.

Filamentous algae – Algae that grow in a hair-like fashion. A nuisance organism that can "choke out" sessile reef animals.

Filter feeders – Organisms that utilize special feeding appendages to strain food from the passing water.

Gobies – Fishes within the family Gobidae.

Grammas – Fishes within the family Grammatidae.

Hermatypic – A term used to describe the animals that house photosynthetic organisms, such as zooxanthellae.

Iodine – A nonmetal minor element. In sea water, iodine is common in two forms: iodide and iodate. Iodine is a very important element to many living organisms.

Kalkwasser – A salt that dissociates into calcium and hydroxide ions. German for "calcium water."

Kelvin rating – An expression of the perceived color being emitted from the bulb while burning compared to a known color/temperature source.

Magnesium – The second most prevalent cation in sea water, with an average concentration of approximately 1,288 parts per million (ppm).

Major elements – Elements that exist in a concentration that is greater than or equal to 1 part per million (ppm) by weight.

Minor elements – Elements that exist in concentrations of less than 1 part per million (ppm) but more than 1 part per billion (ppb) by weight.

Nano-reef – A reef aquarium holding less than 20 gallons (75.6 l) in total volume.

Nematocysts – One of the stinging organelles of coelenterates used in capturing prey.

Nonconservatively – Refers to elements that are utilized by living organisms.

Nutrients – A nutritive substance. Most commonly refers to substances that are required for plant growth.

pH – A measure of acidity and alkalinity of a solution that is a number on a scale on which a value of 7 represents neutrality and lower numbers indicate increasing acidity. Higher numbers indicate increasing alkalinity. Each unit of change on the pH scale represents a tenfold change in acidity or alkalinity that is the effective logarithm of the effective hydrogen-ion concentration or hydrogen-ion activity in gram equivalents per liter of the solution.

Photoperiod – A light cycle that usually consists of 12 hours of light and 12 hours of darkness.

Photosynthesis – Synthesis of chemical compounds with the aid of radiant energy (light). Formation of carbohydrates from carbon dioxide and a source of hydrogen (water) in the chlorophyll-containing tissues of plants exposed to light.

Pipefishes – Fishes within the family Syngnathidae.

Protandrous hermaphroditism – The ability to change sex to either male or female, depending on the need for one or the other within a group of specimen. Most commonly used to describe anemonefishes, born as males, which change sex to female in order to reproduce.

Pseudochromids – Fishes within the family Pseudochromidae.

Reef basslets – Fishes within the family Serranidae.

Salinity – The amount of measurable salts in a liquid. Most commonly measured in units of parts per thousand (ppt).

Seahorses – Fishes within the family Syngnathidae.

Strontium – A soft, malleable ductile element that is in the same group as both calcium and magnesium.

Trace elements – Elements that are present in concentrations of less than or equal to 1 part per billion (ppb).

Wrasses – Fishes within the family Labridae.

Zoanthids – Colorful colonial and solitary polyps that often resemble miniature anemones.

Zooxanthellae – Algae that reside within the membranes of corals and other cnidarians. The algae provide nutrition for the animal in which it resides, while the animal provides protection for the algae.

Bibliography

Delbeek, J. C. and Julian Sprung. 1994. *The Reef Aquarium*. Ricordia Publishing, Coconut Grove, Florida, 544 pp.

Libes, S. M. 1992. *An Introduction to Marine Biogeochemistry*. John Wiley and Sons, Inc., New York, 734 pp.

Meinkoth, N. A. 1995. *National Audubon Society Field Guide to North American Seashore Creatures*. Knopf, New York, 812 pp.

Michael, S. W. 1999. *A PocketExpert Guide to Marine Fishes*. T.F.H. / Microcosm Professional Series, Neptune City, New Jersey, 447 pp.

Michael, S. W. 2001. *Reef Fishes: Volume 1*. T.F.H. / Microcosm Professional Series, Neptune City, New Jersey, 624 pp.

Michael, S. W. 2004. *Angelfishes and Butterflyfishes*. T.F.H. / Microcosm Professional Series, Neptune City, New Jersey, 344 pp.

Michael, S. W. 2004. *Basslets, Dottybacks & Hawkfishes*. T.F.H. / Microcosm Professional Series, Neptune City, New Jersey, 296 pp.

Nybakken, J. W. 1993. *Marine Biology: An Ecological Approach*. Harper Collins, New York, 462 pp.

The Oceanography Course Team. 1999. *Seawater: Its Composition, Properties, and Behavior*. Butterworth-Heinemann, Oxford, 168 pp.

Valiela, I. 1995. *Marine Ecological Processes*. Springer, New York, 686 pp.

Wilkerson, J. D. 1998. *Clownfishes*. T.F.H. / Microcosm Professional Series, Neptune City, New Jersey, 240 pp.

Resources

INTERNET RESOURCES

AquaLink

www.aqualink.com

The largest aquaria web resource in the world, AquaLink provides fishkeepers with information on a variety of topics, including freshwater and marine fish, aquatic plants, goldfish, reef systems, invertebrates, and corals.

Aquaria Central

www.aquariacentral.com

Aquaria Central is an online resource offering species profiles, help forums, chat rooms, and a variety of aquaria articles. To date, there are more than 700 species profiles listed on this website's searchable database.

AquariumHobbyist

www.aquariumhobbyist.com

This website lists upcoming marine-related events, as well as commercial pages, chat rooms, news, a classifieds section, and care information.

Reef Central

www.reefcentral.com

Reef Central is an online community that shares information regarding the marine and reef aquarium hobby. The site includes access to discussion forums, photo galleries, chat rooms, and news.

Reefs.Org

www.reefs.org

An online interactive community, Reefs.Org is home to an active bulletin board, reference library, chat room, monthly periodical, and online curriculum.

Wet Web Media

www.wetwebmedia.com

This website features extensive aquarium, fish, and aquatic information, with numerous articles on marine aquariums, freshwater aquariums, aquarium plants, ponds, and other related topics.

ORGANIZATIONS

The Breeder's Registry
5541 Columbia Drive North
Fresno, CA 93727
E-mail: tlang@aquariusaquarium.org
http://www.breeders-registry.gen.ca.us/index.htm

Federation of American Aquarium Societies (FAAS)
Secretary: Jane Benes
E-mail: Jbenes01@yahoo.com

Federation of British Aquatic Societies (FBAS)
Secretary: Vivienne Pearce
E-mail: Webmaster@fbas.co.uk

The International Federation of Online Clubs and Aquatic Societies (IFOCAS)
E-mail: ifocas@ifocas.fsworld.co.uk
http://www.ifocas.fsworld.co.uk

Marine Aquarium Council (MAC)
923 Nu'uanu Avenue
Honolulu, HI 96817
Telephone: (808) 550-8217
Fax: (808) 550-8317
E-mail: info@aquariumcouncil.org
http://www.aquariumcouncil.org

Marine Aquarium Societies of North America
Director of Membership/Secretary: Cheri Phillips
E-mail: cheri@uniquesensations.com
http://www.masna.org

PUBLICATIONS

Tropical Fish Hobbyist Magazine
1 TFH Plaza
Third & Union Avenues
Neptune City, NJ 07753
For subscription information please visit:
www.tfhmagazine.com
or call: 1-888-859-9034

Photo Credits

Jim Walters provided the reef photograph used on the cover of this book, as well as many others used throughout its pages. A dedicated hobbyist and photographer, Mr. Walters has run Old Town Aquarium in Chicago, Illinois with his business partner, Ian Schakowsky, for nearly 20 years. Old Town Aquarium has proudly displayed, sold and maintained nano-reef aquariums, and many other types, since the early 1980s. For more information, visit www.oldtownaquarium.com.

Author, 23, 26, 29, 31, 33, 36, 40, 47-49, 53, 58-61, 75, 77, 80, 82-83, 107, 119, 145, 149, 163, 166-169
D. Herlong, 56
I. Francais, 79
J. Fatherree, 160
J. Hemdal, 112, 141
L. Leddo, 118
M.P. & C. Piednoir, 6, 16, 21, 34, 46, 52, 64, 69, 78, 86, 99, 121, 123, 126, 131, 154, 161
O. Lucanus, 142
G.W. Lange, 153
M. Smith, 109

E. Taylor, 125
F. Stanislav, 134
R. Nesa, 162
R. Steene, 8, 158
T.F.H. Photo Archives, 8, 10, 14, 17-19, 20, 24, 30, 32, 37-38, 41-43, 44, 50-51, 54, 57, 62, 63, 66-68, 70, 72-74, 76, 81, 85, 88, 90-98, 100-103, 105, 108, 110-111, 114-117, 122, 124, 129-130, 132-133, 135-139, 146-147, 151, 152, 155-157, 159, 164

Additional cover photography courtesy of **Creatas**

183

Resources

Index